THE ONE PAN GOURMET COOKS LITE

A LOW-FAT GUIDE TO OUTDOOR COOKING

by Don Jacobson & Don Mauer

ICS Books Inc.
Merrillville, Indiana

ILLUSTRATIONS by Robin Cook & James Putrus

All ICS titles are published on recycled paper.

Printed in the U.S.A.

PUBLISHED BY:
ICS Books, Inc.
1370 E. 87th Place
Merrillville, IN 46410
800-541-7323

Library Of Congress Cataloguing-in-Publication Data
Jacobson, Donald.
The one pad gourmet cooks lite / by Don Jacobson and Don Mauer.
    p.   cm.
  Includes index.
  ISBN 1-57034-033-1
  1. Outdoor cookery. 2. Low-fat diet--Recipes. I. Mauer . Don.
II Title.
TX823 . J338   1996   96-4043
841 . 5'78--dc20   CIP

In the following chapters, you will find a number of references and tables providing nutritional information. The authors have used the following sources for that information:

The Corrine T. Netzer Encyclopedia of Food Values by Corrine T. Netzer, Dell Books, 1992.

The Dictionary of Calories and Carbohydrates by Barbara Kraus, Grosset & Dunlap, 1973.

Santé (For Good Health) with Joanne Ossell, M.S., R.D., weight control, diet planning, exercise software from Hopkins Technology, Hopkins, Minnesota 55343-7117, 1991.

In addition, *Food & Cooking for Health* by Lawrence E. Lamb (Viking Press, 1973) was a useful resource.

ACKNOWLEDGEMENTS

For me, life on the trail has always been exercise disrupted by setups, tear-downs and meal building. And, the meals have always been more important than the rest.

As the man who inspired me to rethink my outdoor lifestyle, my co-author, Don Mauer, a man who's living "lean and lovin' it!" has proven throughout this collaborative effort to be an ingenious chef and a remarkable human being. A huge portion of this work rests upon his broad and capable shoulders.

I'd like to take a moment to once again thank all of my trail friends who have urged me to continue to compose my outdoor recipes. Every one of them knows who they are. My only regret is that they are a legion too large to mention individually.

Of course, Tom Todd of ICS Books Inc., whose faith when others did not believe that low-fat cookery had a place in the woods, was a constant source of comfort. The work of all the people at ICS have, without a doubt, made this a better work.

Finally, I cannot begin to thank my wife, Pam, and children, Katie and Michael...the three people who always walk with me in fact or thought wherever my trail takes me. Your love and support is boundless.

Don Jacobson
Downers Grove, Illinois
October, 1995

My brothers and my father loved the outdoors and were all big on the Boy Scouts. My dad remained involved with scouting well after his sons' interest had passed. I think what he loved the most was being out of doors, being warmed by the sun, cooking up great chow and spending quality time with his buddies.

I, however, was the complete opposite. I hated camping and cooking outdoors. The very first time I spent a night in a tent, I froze. My teeth chattered almost all night. I hated it. Breakfast was cold cereal, lunch was baloney sandwiches and dinner was burned meat and raw vegetables. For me, it was the "Not-So-Great" outdoors.

My wife Susan loved camping and fishing. She was always willing to get up early on a cool morning and head for the lake with her dad. He was born and raised in northern Wisconsin and loved everything about the outdoors. He instilled that love in his daughter and she, in turn, instilled it in me. Hey, better late than never.

In 1976, my wife and I camped our way across the northern states from Illinois to Oregon and then camped our way down the West Coast till we reached Southern California. We camped in a tent and cooked almost all our meals over an open fire. Believe it or not, I loved it.

Was I cold at night? Sometimes. Were some of the campsite showers cold? Oh, yeah. Did I love the smell of wet pine and the sound of early morning birds? Big time. My love of the outdoors would not have been possible without my wife Susan's love for me.

I would never have thought, back when I was eleven years old, that someday I would have the honor of working with my co-author on a book about how to cook healthy, easy-to-prepare outdoor food. Without Don Jacobson's love of the outdoors and his love for campsite cooking, this book would never have been possible. Thank you both for sharing the joy of the truly great outdoors.

I also wish to thank my cousin, Gayle Jensen, for putting Don Jacobson and me together. For without her doing so, this book would never have been possible.

Don Mauer
Raleigh, North Carolina
October, 1995

TABLE OF CONTENTS

INTRODUCTION

It's remarkable how particular phrases, when delivered by certain people, can really focus your attention.

Like the bureaucrat magnanimously proclaiming, "The government only wants to help you..."

The salesman earnestly vowing, "Trust me..."

The teenager tentatively whispering, "Dad, there's a problem with the car..."

Or, "Mr. Jacobson, we've noticed something unusual on your Thallium treadmill stress test."

All of us reach a point in life when we have to start paying attention to body parts we ignored in our twenties. I thought I had been pretty good at being a responsible adult, giving up fun things like smoking, pitchers of beer, massive doses of cheese and sausage pizza combined with candy bars. So, the call from my doc was a scary surprise.

Besides, I'm an avid outdoorsman...hiking, camping, fishing. I work out regularly. No way my system could be clogged!

Truth was, I was right, at least about my heart. The reading was a false positive caused by my diaphragm obscuring the lower part of the muscle. But, this was a wake-up call to let me know I was not healthy, especially when it came to my approach to food.

Too much fat and sodium. Not enough calories from carbohydrates and protein. It was not a case of fast-food-itis, but rather that all-too-American urge to live well by eating well. And that meant going heavy on oils and cream sauces, relishing richly marbled meats, and so forth. And, as the author of a successful outdoor cookbook, I had created an image of the backcountry chef ready to do battle with freeze-dried boredom.

I was heavy—well-upholstered if you will—(24% body fat) and not going anywhere but up, on the scale, on the cholesterol count, on every risk factor you could imagine. Something had to change. It was going to be the way I looked at food, both at home and on the trail. So, I sat down with my friend Don Mauer, who's living "lean and lovin' it!"

As "the other Don," I've gone through the same process faced by my friend Don J. I've loved cooking since I was 15 years old. I took over the cooking chores two weeks after I was married. Cream, butter, nuts and chocolate made up a major portion of my recipe collection and daily food plan. Back in the early '90s, I weighed in at 308 pounds. My cholesterol was at 260.

A doctor's visit was my wake-up call. He painted a very grim picture of what would happen to me if I did not modify my eating habits immediately. Pictures of heart attacks and worse flickered in a vivid mind movie.

Being relatively intelligent, I listened to the medical man and altered my point-of-view about food. I realized that fat makes you fat. Not pasta, rice or broccoli, but fat. I learned that the American Heart Association recommended no more than 30% of daily calories should come from fat. However, more learned minds than mine had determined that 20% or less daily calories from fat would be of far greater health benefit. So I committed myself to getting no more than 20% of my calories from fat every day.

I knew that there would be no dietician standing over my shoulder. I also knew that whatever I ate had to fit within the context of a healthy, low-fat diet. Ultimately, I discovered that you could be honest to both yourself and the food you prepared. You just had to approach your resources sensibly, recognizing that one meal was part of a whole day's-worth of meals. That's exactly how I lost over 100 pounds.

It is not remarkable that the medical community urges people to emphasize a low-fat, low-sodium lifestyle combined with exercise. That means getting outdoors, hiking, camping, kayaking, cycling. What is extraordinary is that often, the moment we step outside, we consume high-sodium, suspect-tasting, freeze-dried concoctions or stoke up on convenience foods like cold cuts, burgers and hot dogs.

There is a better way.

Now, we won't argue with our ridge-running comrades who are out in the hills for the long haul. They have to go the freeze-dried or the fruit-nut-grain and dried veggie-pasta route. There is definitely room for that in an exciting low-fat outdoor menu. But, you can live well on the trail and follow a low-fat food plan at the same time.

We know. We've done it.

Traveling Lite, But Well, On The Trail

Get off your duff and get on the trail, road or river. That's the best prescription a doctor can give a Baby Boomer—male or female. We know we need to exercise more and eat smarter. Hips and thighs revealed to the world in all their Spandex-wrapped glory bring an enlightened knowledge of the forehead-slapping, cringing sort.

In that blinding moment of revelation, we know we need to get the old internal fires burning hotter to melt off the lard and tighten up the muscles we've ignored in our quest for success. We know that no matter how hard we try, that last five...or fifteen pounds...will be impossible to lose simply by wishing. We know that we have to get fit or stay fat.

Full of new resolve, we rush off to the local outfitter and drop some Ben Franklins on the latest gear. Then we plan a trip. Just a few short days in the country. And, of course, we have to go to the store to shop for food for the weekend. Something easy...something tasty...something probably loaded with fat and sodium.

That's the contradiction in the crusade to get trim. We're all pretty good about cutting fat out of the meals we eat at home, but the moment we head outside, our conviction evaporates. Maybe we think it's too hard to cook lighter on the trail. Maybe we are unconsciously compensating for the hard work of kayaking by "treating" ourselves. Maybe we are rationalizing by saying, "I'll burn it off." Or, maybe we just don't know any better.

Whatever the reasons, you're sure to sabotage your best efforts to firm up through exercise and hard work by eating the wrong foods.

Dieticians will start you on the road to better eating by reducing calories and by limiting your fat calories (one gram of fat contains nine calories) to less than 30% of that total. That's smart, whether you need to lose weight or not. But, if you want to drop a few pounds, you have to cut your fat intake even further and increase your exercise regimen. People of the human persuasion require about 12 calories per day per pound to maintain weight. So, if you weigh 150 pounds, you'll need about 1,800 calories.

But, if 140 pounds—and not 150—is your healthiest weight, you should do two things. First, take in the same amount of calories you would if you weighed 140 pounds. Using the aforementioned calculation (12 x 140), you would have to take in 1,680 calories instead of 1,800. If you took in only 1,300, you'd lose weight faster, right? Not likely. You're dealing with a case of the unconscious mind over matter.

Current research indicates that even if you have decided that 140 pounds is your healthiest weight, taking in fewer than 1,680 calories may be misinterpreted. Your survival centers will conclude that you are starving. Your body, heedless of well-intentioned weight loss efforts, will then slow your metabolism to conserve calories. The wisest rule is to consume the ideal amount of calories every day.

Second, break out those 1,680 calories in such a way as to get 20% or less of them from fat. That would mean, for this example, you would get 336 calories from fat (1,680 x 0.20). How many fat grams is that? 336 calories ÷ 9 calories per gram, or 37 fat grams.

Both authors are examples of exactly how well this system works. You'll get enough calories so your body will not think it's starving, and you'll reduce your fat intake to a very healthy level.

One word of caution: Do as we did. Make an appointment with your doctor or health care professional. Discuss your goals and plans with them. Chances are excellent they will applaud your decision and assist you in attaining your goal. Your physician knows your health history and can make the proper call. Don't let any book be the last word. Include your doctor in the decision-making process.

Let's be clear about one thing, though, before we go any further. We are not suggesting that you go out "mudding" it with the expressed intent of losing weight over the weekend instead of losing it all week. Deprivation dieting is probably more foolhardy on the trail than at home because you are demanding a lot more of your body. There is no way you will have an enjoyable outdoor experience if you are hungry, worn out or just plain sore.

What's Food Got To Do With It?

Earlier, we talked about how you need enough calories to keep you going over the hill and the dale. Truth is, humans can take in energy without a lot of fuss or ritual. The pilot who was shot down over Bosnia discovered that ants taste a bit like lemon, only crunchier. If we are forced to, we can strip enough bark, grub up enough berries and catch enough fish, fowl and rodents to help us survive in the outdoors in the harshest circumstances.

Our game, though, is not to survive, but to thrive.

We go outdoors to test ourselves against challenges...climbing a 300-foot cliff face, hiking a section of the John Muir Trail or cycling along 32 miles of central Illinois highway. We are not attempting to reawaken the primal human within us that has been buried for about 200 generations.

Trail meals complement our total experience. They provide the energy we require to replace stores depleted. But, these repasts also have an aesthetic role that enhances the effort made earlier in the day. There is nothing better than to look out over a glistening pond, burning orange in "Golden Time," while enjoying a plate full of Pasta Primavera laced with marinated chicken.

Aesthetics of a more internalized nature also play a role in the meals we eat. We eat to replace lost energy. We have to assume that the more we eat, the more energy we gain. If we do not find the food appealing, we'll eat less of it and, therefore, replace less energy. Eventually, that will put us behind the eight ball.

A final justification for the creation of a great meal after a hard day is a bit more mystical, but we think valid, nonetheless. It rises from something resonating deep within us.

Recall that after Prometheus stole fire from the gods, he had to have a cage to put it in. That cage was the hearth. Throughout civilization, the human tribe has gathered around the focal point of the home...the hearth. Whether a circle of stones or a medley of electronics, the hearth has always been the center from which we leave satisfied and warm and to which we return seeking nourishment, safety and companionship.

Trekkers of all sorts understand the concept of the hearth. A 40-mile leg of a cycling trip done in a cold drizzle or a stretch of Class 5+ water accomplished in a kayak needs closure beyond the immediate end of the effort. These feats demand a retelling that allows the narrator to relive the experience through the imagination of others. And, although the hearth may be a single burner stove, it will continue to be that place where humanity spends precious moments...never to be recaptured in the same manner again...to pause to recreate triumphs and tragedies.

Why rush away quickly? That's why we fled the canyons of steel and their demands in the first place. Take the few minutes you need to build a meal you will like, one that will replenish the body and help you nourish the soul.

The 2,500 Calorie Dilemma

Men may need 2,500-or-more calories a day to maintain an energy level consistent with increased activity demanded by hearty trekking. Women require somewhat less, but still much more than they regularly take in. You also want to remain consistent with the dietary philosophy you have established within your daily life. If you are low-fat at home, you want to remain low-fat on the trail.

But, reality checks in if you go overboard to eliminate the spare tire. A 35-pound pack will weigh a lot more on Sunday if you've starved yourself on Saturday.

That's because activities like hiking, cycling, canoeing and kayaking go beyond fun and actually become work—work for the body on a level that exceeds appropriate energy depletion to promote weight loss. Work that makes you ache. Work that leaves muscles calling out for replacement protein and new fuel.

You have to walk a fine line between getting trim and getting sick. Don't cut calories and radically increase the exercise load at the same time...especially on a trek. Personal experience shows that lugging a canoe and a 30-pound Duluth pack over a 100-rod portage will contribute to weight loss even with 1,000 calories taken in at each meal. If you hold your intake to 2,000 or 2,500 over the day, you may discover a pleasingly significant reduction in waist and thigh lines.

We've all been around this type of "outdoorsman." You know, the one who buys a six-pack, some cold cuts and bread, and he's ready for the road! True, you can pick up 2,500 calories by eating five bologna sandwiches (yuk!) in a day.

Bologna Sandwich

Item	Calories/Serving	Fat/Serving	Total Cal/Fat
Meat x 3	90 (slice)	8 grams	270/24
Bread	80 (slice)	1 gram	160/2
Miracle Whip®	70 (1 tbsp)	7 grams	70/7
		Grand Total	500/33

If you somehow ate nearly a pound of bologna, you would manage to generate 1,485 calories from fat...60% of your daily calorie demand. A chest-clutcher, for sure! It's even worse when you figure that of the bologna's 120 grams of fat, 50 grams are derived from saturated fat. Saturated fat has been linked to many health problems. Why foul up a good thing with a meal dripping in grease?

On the other hand, you could create a wonderful calorie-packed meal that is also worthy of the "low-fat" label. According to the federal Food and Drug Administration,such a meal generates 30% or fewer of its total calories from fat. Look at this sample recipe.

Primary Poulet & Pasta

½ skinless boneless chicken breast (about 4 oz.), cut into chunks
1 tablespoon olive oil
1 lemon, juiced
¼ teaspoon dried basil, oregano, black pepper and garlic powder
salt to taste (optional)

1 medium sweet green pepper, diced
1 medium sweet red pepper, diced
1 carrot, peeled and diced
½ cup baby spring peas
1 cup precooked macaroni
1 tablespoon grated Parmesan cheese

In a bowl, mix oil, spices, salt and pepper and lemon juice. Add chicken and stir together. Cover and let sit for ten minutes. Over medium flame, heat pot and place chicken in to brown and cook. Tend regularly to avoid burning. Reserve marinade. When chicken is white throughout (10 to 15 minutes), add oil and spices to pan. Put all vegetables in the pot and saute for two to three minutes only. Add macaroni and warm for one minute more. Remove from heat and add cheese. Toss to mix.

All told, including prep time, this dish takes about 35 to 45 minutes to make in one pan. A lot more appetizing than mystery meat on bread. And a lot better for you. How much better? Let's look at the numbers and see.

Primary Poulet & Pasta

Item	Calories	Fat (grams)
1 medium green pepper	13	0.1
1 medium red pepper	19	0.1
1 medium carrot	25	0.1
½ cup baby peas	58	0.1
2 teaspoons olive oil	83	9.0 (1.2 saturated)
1 C Cooked Macaroni	220	0.9
½ chicken breast	124	1.6 (0.4 saturated)
1 Tbsp Parmesan cheese	23	1.5 (0.1 saturated)
Total	565	13.4

Remember that these are ideal figures and could vary somewhat depending upon raw materials. Talk about some good eating, though! Only 21.3% of this dish's 565 calories (13.4 grams x 9 cal/gram = 120.6 calories) come from fat. You are getting 65 more calories than a bologna sandwich with 19.6 fewer grams of fat! By comparison, a one cup serving of a freeze-dried rice and chicken entree weighs in at just 400 calories of which 29.3% of the calories come from fat. You can max a Primary Poulet meal at more than 800 calories by adding two slices of bread (140 calories, 2 grams fat) and an apple (81 calories, 0.5 grams fat). Overall, you'll get 18.2% of your calories from fat. Do that three times a day (2,400 calories and 47.7 fat grams total), and you'll really be ready to travel. We wouldn't call that deprivation dining, would you?

Putting It All In One Pot, Pan, Or Oven

We go outside because it is so much better than staring at four walls. But why do so many of us also accept that trekking meals have to be boring, tasteless, high-fat or so completely compromised by dried foods or other "demands" of the trail as to become only slightly better than the culinary delights offered up by the fine folks at NASA? You can and should eat as well outside as when you are seated at the dinner table at home.

Trekkers do have to face a few, sometimes painful, facts. They have to lug, pedal or paddle their food wherever they go. They are bound by space limitations, whether found in a backpack, tied to the thwart in a canoe or hanging from the panniers of a bicycle. The effects of size and weight ceilings increase directly with the number of days and nights to be spent on the trail. Long-haul trekkers, without doubt, have to concentrate calories whenever possible.

But, most of us head out late Friday and return sometime on Sunday. Two nights at most, with either four or five meals in the package.

The weekend trekker can think more about nutrition and aesthetics while concentrating less on weight and space, although these factors cannot be ignored altogether. A Dutch oven still will not pack well during a New Hampshire Presidential transit. On the other hand, within the context of a 30 pound pack, a smart camper can devote considerable space to food and assorted condiments by carefully planning cooking gear requirements.

That's the essence of "The One Pan" philosophy. *Reduce the hardware...increase the foodware and the fun!*

You can eat well by using fresh foods and just one pot, pan or backpack oven. And, you can eat lean while enjoying every bite. All you have to do is realize that eating is part of living...and the best living is on the trail.

Truth is, by not bringing your skillet, you may only save a few ounces in overall pack weight. Yet, trekkers are always being pushed to save ounces and pounds by substituting freeze-dried "convenience" foods (that demand substantial quantities of water for rehydration) for fresh. Let's put the shoe on the other foot in a sort of "Chef's Revenge" (as in "living well is the best...") and lose the metal in favor of a low-fat cuisine based upon fresh foods.

Another big plus? Fresh foods are less expensive than those aluminum-foiled, freeze-dried packets.

Besides, how much does a decent 800-calorie meal of fresh foods really weigh? A pound?

We're talking about a mindset...one that demands a degree of precision in meal-planning. This ethic calls for the trekker to become as aware of the fuel needed to succeed in the quest as he or she is of the voyage itself. It pushes for an appreciation of the fact that a key part of the outdoor experience is one that can be controlled. All it requires is some thought about what foods will be needed and what vessel(s) will be called for to cook these meals. The discipline to leave equipment behind is part of the focusing effort.

Even the equipment you do bring can contribute to just how low-fat your meals will be. For instance, a non-stick skillet eliminates the need for oils as lubrication. You may still want small amounts of oil (like olive) for flavoring. Oil becomes a seasoning, not a necessity. Kiss that margarine good-bye as well. A level tablespoon of the yellow goo contains 100 calories, of which 99 are from fat.

You shouldn't spend all your time on technique. It's the substance...and subsistence...that's the meat of the matter. The food is the focus of a One Pan menu, Lite or otherwise.

The primary goal of any outdoor menu is to insure that you are fed and re-energized. The secondary objective is to get your energy in a healthy manner. That demands thought on your part, a level of consideration that goes beyond rushing to the store on Friday afternoon and loading your shopping cart with whatever is handy or easy.

You check your tent for leaks before you leave because you don't want to get wet, right? You should build meals with the idea that you don't want to go hungry. The next chapter will teach you how.

Meal Building: Making The Sum Greater Than The Parts

This is not "Nutrition 101."

Any diet designed to meet your nutritional requirements has to be balanced. A trail diet, low-fat or not, has to give you what your body needs to stay healthy and run well or it's wrong no matter how "healthy" you think it may be. That means you have get your measure of protein, carbohydrates, vitamins, minerals, and, yes, fat. But, too little or too much of any element can be a problem. Too little is self-explanatory. Too much is the fight modern man faces.

The weird thing about the human body is that it is still in many ways a prehistoric organic machine. Our bodies operate like we are still loping across the sere plains of Kenya with days between water holes and meals. Then, as now, we need to be fit to survive. And, our bodies are ingenious when it came to preserving themselves.

When times were flush, the body stored excess calories in the form of fat. When times were lean, the body lived off the reserves previously locked away on butt, gut, hips and thighs. Worked great when all we had were patches of wild grain or fruits and the remains of an occasional lion kill that hadn't been stripped by the hyenas.

Anthropologists and archaeologists can tell you how much time our species devoted to food gathering some 120 centuries ago. We can't. But, you can be sure that it was a big chunk of every day. Food gathering was the numero uno priority. Today, we can walk into a fast food joint and go face down in 1,200 calories in a matter of five minutes. Then, food was a necessity, the object of everyday existence. Now, we have been relieved of that burden to allow ourselves to concentrate on more important things...like dieting.

You see, in this day and age, when even the government does its best to guarantee all comers three squares a day, our industrious metabolism digests only so many calories, leaving a lot of the rest to be stored away where they are most embarrassingly visible. And, not all of this padding comes from french fries. You can get fat from carbohydrates as well as fat. All it takes is to consume more carbohydrate calories than we burn, and our bodies will automatically store the excess as fat, just in case a lean time comes up.

Here's another thought...we need protein to help build and rebuild muscle, bone, blood cells and skin. Protein is also a source of energy. Most experts think that the body needs somewhere around 280 protein calories per day to repair and replenish as well as fuel the fire. At 4 calories per gram of protein, that means we need about 70 grams of protein from various sources, either vegetable or animal, per day. Any more than that, except in high-activity scenarios like hiking, camping and cycling, and the body will convert a healthy portion of the excess into fat. Shades of the savannah! Another problem is that many high protein foods can also be high in fat. You can get a great 64.3 gram protein blast from a 10 ounce slab of roasted choice prime rib, but you also get an artery-choking 90.5 grams of fat. The protein will supply 257 calories but the fat drags another 815 calories along. Yikes.

This chart illustrates how we have to be careful when selecting protein sources. The difference between extra lean hamburger and sirloin tip is instructive, but not astonishing. What we can learn is how processing and packaging can take a hidden toll on our diets. First and foremost, to process meats, salt often is added to preserve the meat. Other flavor enhancements also are included that may actually increase the fat content to improve the flavor of lesser cuts used by meat packers.

Protein Sources

Food	Protein (grams/calories)	Fat (grams/calories)
4 oz. lean raw hamburger	21.2/84.8	19.2/172.8
4 oz. raw sirloin tip	23.2/92.8	1.2/10.8
4 oz. raw beaver	27.2/108.8	5.6/50.4
1 oz. cheddar cheese	7.1/28.4	9.4/84.6
½ c. cottage cheese	14.1/56.4	5.1/45.9
5 oz. canned chicken w/broth	30.9/123.6	11.3/101.7
4 oz. roast chicken, light meat	30.8/123.2	4.6/41.4
4 oz. raw barley	14.0/56.0	2.8/25.2
1 c. boiled red kidney beans	41.4/165.6	0.2/1.8
1 medium avocado	4.0/16.0	30.8/277.2
Freeze-dried chick/rice entree	13.0/52.0	13.0/117.0

In previous outdoor cookbooks, it was suggested to use canned meats as an alternative to fresh-frozen meat in certain situations. Yet, a five-ounce can of chicken with broth contains nearly three times as much fat as a piece of fresh skinless, boneless chicken breast. Forget that recommendation. As for the freeze-dried chicken and rice entree, recall that it generates just under 30% of its calories from fat (29.3%), barely enough to qualify as low-fat. Recall also that its total calorie count was about 400. You would still need to bring in another 400 calories to make an 800-calorie meal a reality. And, that attempt could likely throw the meal into fat city.

Another reason excess fat in the menu is a problem rests in the way the body converts food to energy. Like any good salesman, the body goes where the action is, incinerating food calories from sources that are easiest to digest. At the top of the short list are carbohydrates (grains, beans and greens are super carbo sources). Fats (some from vegetables, seeds and nuts, but mostly animal), on the other hand, are the most difficult to burn and often end up moving directly from the alimentary canal to the beltline overlap.

That's because fats take the longest to digest. Think of your digestive tract like a line waiting to get Rolling Stones tickets. Up at the front are carbos and proteins. Fats (as always, it seems) bring up the rear. If the body gets the bulk of its energy from converting carbos first and then protein, many of the fat calories will be in excess of the body's daily need. Guess what happens then?

To avoid that eventuality, the low-fat mission should be to keep total fat intake throughout the day *at or near 20% of calories.* For a 2,500 calorie-per-day food plan, that means a fat maximum of 56 grams or 500 fat calories. How we fill out the other 1,990 will be the next subject of attention.

Meal Building: A Daily Question Of Balance

You can boil (pun alert!) a 2,500 calorie food plan down to a simple mathematical statement:

500 (fat cals) + 280 (protein cals) + ? (carbo cals) = 2,500

For the calculator-impaired, the answer is 1,720 carbohydrate calories.

You do need to have a portion of all three energy sources within food to maintain a proper diet. The above equation is based upon the idea that a 20% fat calorie level is the maximum acceptable guideline. You or your doctor may think otherwise. No argument from these quarters. If you want to reduce fat calories further, you can increase carbohydrate calories. And, given that we are suggesting food ideas for outdoor activities, you could increase the protein count to a certain extent without concern.

A note before we go on: In spite of the best intentions, you may be shortchanging your body by making some food choices over others. We suggest you use an appropriate supplementary multivitamin supplement simply as a precaution.

There is a problem of sorts inherent in food in its natural, raw state. Unlike a clinic or laboratory, your outdoor kitchen is going to be involved in preparing foods that are a combination of carbohydrate, fat and protein calorie sources (as well as being chock full of essential vitamins and minerals). As we have seen (remember the prime rib?), foods that are an excellent source of one factor may be disastrous when it comes to another. You have to consider the whole food when you are building a meal.

A bit of practical advice (avocados, with 30 fat grams in each one, notwithstanding): If it grows from a seed, it will usually be low in fat, high in fiber and carbohydrates, and, except for legumes (beans), a moderate source of protein. Food that hoofs it to your pot, pan or oven demands greater attention, offering excellent protein levels while possibly being rule-busting fat calorie source.

But, we aren't so obsessive about when or how you take in those 500-or-so fat calories. We believe it's where you are at the end of the day that counts...not at each stop along the way. Let prudence be your guide.

For instance, you may like to start your day off with ham and eggs backed up by some fruit and toast. A 1.5 ounce slice of roasted ham shank, properly trimmed, gives you 9.4 grams of fat. Two large eggs, scrambled, are good for 15 grams of fat. Two slices of toast with margarine will add another 9.3 grams of fat, while an orange is a negligible 0.2 grams. You've put about 34 grams of fat on your daily account of 56 grams...more than half. The meal, you'll agree, is definitely not low-fat (under 30% calories from fat). Let's revisit those items on the morning menu.

Ham & Eggs Breakfast

	Total Calories	Calories From Fat
1.5 oz. ham	129	84.6
2 large eggs	202	135.0
2 slices wheat bread	140	18.0
2 tsp. margarine	66	65.7
1 medium orange	62	1.8
Total	599	305.1(50.9%)

You certainly could be smarter, but the meal is probably more of a sodium (if you use canned ham) nightmare than it is a dilemma in the low-fat outdoor world. You could eliminate some of those fat calories by using an egg substitute and eating your toast dry or with a butter-flavored non-fat spread.

Enjoy your breakfast, but realize that your dinner, in particular, will often end up being a meal that will feature more fat calories. Thus, you have to watch what you do the rest of the day. You don't want to go over the top of the fat wall by nightfall.

If you go big at breakfast, you will, therefore, have to look closely at what you plan to eat for snacks, lunch and, most important, the finale for the day of hard trekking, dinner. That delightful pasta with cream sauce supper may have to be replaced with something else. Perhaps you might bend over your camp stove and make a chicken breast browned with fresh basil and garlic on a non-stick pan and then poached in white wine accompanied by some precooked baby carrots, fresh corn cut from the cob and sliced zucchini browned with a dash of olive oil in the pan after the chicken and wine are removed. Remember, you get to drink the rest of the wine with dinner. Adding rice or beans or pasta will get those calories to 800, while adding very little fat.

Snacks are another important consideration. Since your body prefers to use the food you eat today for today's energy supply, the breakfast you eat at 7 A.M. could be burned up by 10 A.M.

Late afternoon is another time your body may have completely converted its most recent fuel load, lunch, into useable energy. You could crash without another little power boost to kick you back into high gear until the next meal. That's why we suggest a late morning and late afternoon snack.

It could be something as easy as a banana (105 cals/26.7 grams of carbohydrate/0.6 grams of fat) or as crunchy as a half-cup of low-fat granola with raisins and almonds (210 cals/40 grams carbo/3 grams of fat). The key is to keep the carbohydrate calorie count up because that is what you need...a quick energy burst...while staying within the fat guidelines of 20% or less.

A chunk of beef stick is a tasty snack, but concentrates far too many of its calories in the fat part of the wheel. Those calories will be more difficult to utilize in your system. That will deny you the boost you need to help you get to the next stage of your trip. And, watch out for nuts and coconut meat. While they offer protein and lots of carbos, they are also loaded with fat. GORP (good old raisins and peanuts) can get you. Be smart about your snacks.

A Time To Eat...A Time To Refrain From Eating

The diet doctors have been saying for years that farmers and diabetics have had it right all along. Eat big at the top of the day, lighter at the end of the day. Don't eat a meal shortly before going to bed. There is logic here. If you are going to be working hard throughout the day, it's only reasonable that you stoke up your furnace with good, high-calorie meals. At the far end, after all the work is done, you can reasonably replace lost protein and refill the tank without a huge meal. And, when your body drops into neutral overnight, the last thing you want is to be converting food into unwanted calories. Guess where cheese and crackers end up (besides becoming crumbs in your sleeping bag)?

Over the past fifty years, we have changed the way we eat in our regular lives. Now, breakfast is eaten on the run. Lunch is grabbed wherever and whenever. By default, dinner has become the main family meal and is a big one. We are not going to suggest any lifestyle alterations for outdoor eating that you are not making Monday through Friday.

Yet, since we are not planning your outdoor menus for you, all we can do (besides help you make your meals as interesting as possible) is give you a few pointers on when we think you might want to position certain calorie sources.

For instance, since fat calories take the body the longest to convert into energy, consider keeping the majority of the 56 grams of fat taken within the 2,500 calorie menu at the front end of the day. You could then reserve less than a third for the dinner meal. Recall that *Primary Poulet* (see pages 6, 7) provided just under than 18 grams of fat. The full 800-calorie dinner we discussed contained about 20 grams of fat. That leaves 34 grams for breakfast, lunch and snacks. Ham and egg substitute...here we come!

On the contrary, you could bank your protein for later, say dinner, to replenish muscle tissues broken down during the day's exercise.

As for carbos...they fit well any time, but really fit the best at lunch and snacks.

The key is to maintain your energy level to keep you walking, cycling, kayaking or climbing. And, by keeping your stomach filled with taste-tempting foods, you'll fulfill a psychological need, as well. You won't be as likely to sneak that milk chocolate bar with almonds (1.45 ounces/230 cals/14 grams of fat—55% calories from fat) before zipping up the tent flap for the night if you've satisfied your taste buds throughout the day.

SUPERMARKET SWEEP:
THE COMMON SENSE GUIDE TO
FILLING YOUR PACK

We are surrounded by convenience foods from morning through night. But, while these foods may be convenient to prepare, they most certainly can be inconvenient for a person who is paying attention to either fat or sodium.

Here's a favorite. All of us want to start the day with a good breakfast—something that will give us lots of energy to put a lot of ground behind us. So, we turn to that old standby, oatmeal. It's easy to cook. You can dress it up with fruit and sugar...even a touch of nuts. And, oatmeal is packed with carbos ready to fire up a trekker's legs, arms and back. No cholesterol. Limited amount of fat. A virtuous meal. So, you boil some water, reach into the larder for a packet of instant oatmeal...

Stop right there. There's a hidden surprise. Turn the instant packet over and check the food facts. Then compare it to a container of regular oatmeal. A ⅔-cup serving of Quaker Old Fashioned Oatmeal® has 99 calories/18.6 grams carbo/2 grams fat, while a packet of Instant Quaker has 94 calories/18 grams carbo/2 grams fat. No difference, true; until you get to the sodium column: Quaker Old Fashioned: 1 mg. sodium; Quaker Instant: 270 mg. sodium.

You'll find that most brands of instant cereal will have added sodium (salt) when compared to the raw form of the grain to be cooked.

How much time would you have saved by boiling the water and making a packet of oatmeal? Ten minutes? Maybe five? Unless you're rushing to catch the only ferry back to the mainland, that time won't matter. Get up a few minutes earlier.

This is not to say that you should not use food products that have added sodium or fat. On the contrary, you may decide that you want instant oatmeal. That's fine, as long as you take that sodium into account as part your day's allotment, especially if you're on a controlled sodium regimen.

Extra salt or fat is often added to many prepared and packaged foods for a variety of reasons known only to the product creators. It's probably better that we don't know the real reasons. The motive does not matter. The fact that these dietary items are in many of the foods found on our stores' shelves is enough.

A general rule of thumb (unless the label indicates otherwise) is that the sodium content of a packaged food will be higher than the raw version. For instance, take a cup of diced roast ham shank. With 411 calories and 29 grams of fat, this is no bargain. But, it also has just 83 milligrams of sodium, barely a blip on the daily register. Compare that to a cup of canned ham. The canned ham is "leaner," with "just" 317 calories and "only" 21.3 grams of fat. But, a slice of this stuff could be used to patch Utah's Bonneville Salt Flats. One cup of canned ham features 1,317 milligrams of sodium, over half the recommended daily level. So, it's a good idea to learn how to read the nutritional labeling that our friends at the FDA and FTC have so diligently prepared. Be sure to bring a calculator.

Even though the new labeling laws are pretty comprehensive, they still leave a lot to be desired. Did you know that the nutritional fact label can state, per serving, that the fat amount is zero even when there is 0.5 gram? It's true...and legal. However, it's not as factual as we would like.

Look at the top of any nutritional fact label. You'll see the amount of total calories and fat calories. However, in no place on the label are you told what percentage of calories come from fat. Don't be fooled by these labels. There is a percentage calculation for fat, but it's deceptive unless you know what that "9%" or "12%" really mean. What it does not mean is that 9% of the calories are generated by fat.

Simply put, the percentage of fat listed on the label refers to the fat supplied by a single serving of the food product when taken in the context of a 2,000 calorie food plan. Most times, that number (since it refers to the amount of fat in a day) will make the percentage of fat in the product seem artificially small. You'll have to use a calculator to determine the percentage, or use the rule of thumb that we use.

A gram of fat has nine calories. Right? Round it to ten calories, instead. Now assume you're trying to get 20% of your daily calories from fat. That means you can have two grams of fat per 100 calories and stay right where you aim to stay.

When you're shopping, check out the fat grams. Let's say the package you pick up says 5.6 grams of fat per serving. It also states that total calories are 200. Would this fit in a 20% calories from fat plan? At two grams per 100 calories, the answer is no, since this product would have more than 20% (actually 25.2%).

Food For Thought

Sometimes you can maintain many of your regular eating habits by modifying the products you use. For instance, whenever eggs are called for in any of the following recipes, we recommend a nonfat egg substitute (such as the Egg Beaters brand). For home use, we suggest purchasing fresh eggs and separating the white from the yolk. Use the white for cooking and discard the yolk. Why? The yolk is where all the fat is located. Using fresh eggs also costs half as much as frozen nonfat egg substitutes. However, when you're on the trail, refrigeration is non-existent. Therefore, due to the problems with salmonella bacteria and eggs, you'll want to carry a nonfat egg substitute, since it has been pasteurized. The pasteurization process has effectively killed any salmonella bacteria and therefore it won't be a trail problem.

We think beans are great. And not because they are the musical fruit. Legumes of all sorts are a great source of protein and complex carbohydrates, as well as fiber. Most beans are very low in fat. If you plan to use canned beans for your journey, check the sodium content. Some beans have had a lot of salt added to them. If available, use low-sodium beans. Too much salt can make you thirsty on the trail, and the only water you may have is the water you are carrying.

Dried fruits are excellent trail food. They have had much of the water removed and yet are a great source of carbohydrates, vitamins and minerals. They are lightweight (a pound of raisins is a lot of dried grapes), nutritious, and won't spoil on the trail. While shopping, select raisins or dates, dried figs or dried apricots, or even dried cherries, dried strawberries or dried blueberries. All these and more are available—healthy, low-fat and lightweight. What a deal.

Pasta and rice are two excellent lightweight companions for the trail. Yes, they need water in which to cook, but they are easy to carry. Pasta can be cooked and drained in advance of your trip. Place the pasta in a resealable plastic bag and refrigerate. It'll keep just fine for a day or so on the trail. White rice cooks in just 17 minutes and the Minute Rice brand cooks in a flash. No need to cook it ahead. Toss it in the dish you are preparing for an evening meal and let it simmer along with everything else. It'll keep those calories where you want them without bringing any fat along. Truly great trail food.

Touring the aisles of your local supermarket a few days before your trip can be a fun experience, perusing labels as you go. If you want to cut down on your reading and increase your buying, go fresh. By that we mean fresh fruits and vegetables, whole or minimally processed grains like rice, barley, oats or wheat, and non-preserved, non-prefrozen or canned meats.

The wonderful thing about fresh foods is that man has not really gotten his hooks into them yet. What sodium there is, is there because the plant put it there. Fat has not been added to improve the flavor. If you take a piece of meat and carefully and closely trim off any visible fat, you'll go a long way to making your trek leaner.

Every chef will tell you that fresh is best for the aesthetics of taste and texture.

Of course, by eliminating the packaging, you don't have to carry out the waste. Mother Nature is a pretty smart lady.

Getting Loaded

As we said earlier, preparing your outdoor menu is sort of like walking on a balance beam. A little too much of a good thing, one way or the other, and you'll end up giving a new definition to "sticking your landing." That covers the food. But, part of planning your three or four meals goes beyond nutrition. It involves the rough practicalities that comprise the setting for your trip.

How far do you plan to trek during the 40-odd hours from Friday P.M. to Sunday noon? Are you taking a ten-mile walk to and from a shelter? Or are you pedaling from West Yellowstone to Jackson Lake?

What's the terrain going to be? Will you be setting up your stove on a picnic table in the Indiana Dunes or trying to balance it on a rock behind a boulder on Mt. Madison?

What's the weather going to be? A day that warrants a Chicago "heat emergency" calls for different food storage arrangements than snowshoeing along the Pemigewasset in March.

All of these situations have common-sense answers. Taking a long bike trek? Select foods that pack a high-carbo punch into a small amount of space. If you are going to be cooking in extreme conditions on a mountainside, you may want to use simpler recipes that get the food done fast with less fuss. If temperatures are going to soar, the chances of bacterial growth and food spoilage will too. Think about irradiated meats or skip meat altogether and go vegetarian for a few days.

In general, you should be able to carry enough fresh food to cover the type of trip most of us take. For a backpacker or a cyclist who needs to concentrate on saving space, repackaging foods and condiments/spices needed for meals will help reduce excess baggage. Other trekkers probably don't need to repackage, but why carry stuff you don't need?

The easiest way to tackle the problem is to plan your menu, buy the food and then lay out everything on your table. Well, everything except the meat. Pre-cut the portion you need, slice/dice/chunk it, wrap it in foil and freeze it solid. All other ingredients of the recipes you've selected should now face some serious scrutiny.

At your left hand should be the recipe(s). At your right, measuring spoons/cups, vials, plastic baby bottles and food storage (plastic) bags. Ration out what you need into the appropriate container, then add a touch for "breakage." Seal the bag or plastic bottle and stick on a label identifying it and the meal it belongs to. Put everything else away in the pantry.

Beyond repackaging, the One Pan trekker should consider a few other shortcuts to make outdoor cooking easier. Precook rice and pasta at home, and rinse with hot water once cooked, to reduce the possibility of sticking. Pack in a food storage bag to be reheated later within the context of your meal.

Many of the items you'll pack can be loaded into your "outdoor kitchen." There are a couple on the market today that allow the trekker to build a small spice rack, repackage a few oils and keep some essential utensils all in a handy zippered pouch. Of course, you may want to build a more extensive collection of spices. For that, use film canisters. They're watertight and will hold generous portions of seasoned salts, herbs and spices. Use white adhesive tape to label everything.

Packing on Friday should be as easy as pulling the meat from the freezer, double-wrapping it in foil and loading it along with all the other ingredients into a Tupperware bread box, which we've found fits pretty well into a standard backpack and keeps the food protected from shock and dirt. Cyclists will probably hand load their pannier packs. Paddlers will discover that their Duluth sacks offer more liberal storage options.

Of Fire And Iron

Forget every pre-conceived notion you've ever had about camp cookery and flames. Consign images of crackling fires to faded postcards and old John Wayne movies. Low-impact outdoor lifestyles have forced a re-assessment of traditional approaches to camping. The stripping of our forests helped, too.

There's a huge variety of backpacking and portable stoves available to the trekker. For heat control and load-bearing stability, we've found the various Peak One® stoves produced by Coleman really fit the bill. Some models operate on white gas, which is the same as that used for Coleman lanterns. Others are multi-fuel capable, although we'd strongly suggest staying away from unleaded gasoline...too explosive. Other backpacking stoves manufactured by Optimus® and MSR® to name a few, are also good. The stove you select should match the type of trekking and the style of cooking you plan to do. Consult a reputable outdoor retailer for advice.

As for pots and pans...low-fat cooking demands some consideration when it comes to the skillet, at least. Since we are trying to reduce unnecessary fat grams in our outdoor diet, a good place to start is to eliminate the grease we use to keep our meals from becoming too intimate with the hot iron of a standard skillet. For that, we'd suggest using a non-stick pan, covered in Silverstone® or another very durable non-stick coating. A thicker-bottomed skillet tends to burn food less easily than a very thin-bottomed pan. Aluminum is the metal of choice, since it is lightweight and durable.

Another possible area of concern is that the high surface temperatures of most frying pans can kick the fat into a carcinogenic mode. As with most medical reports, studies are not totally conclusive, but are indicative of tendencies. Another reason to be on the safer side.

Any diameter of fry pan will do, although a pan about eight inches across should give you more than enough room to cook a wonderful meal. Don't go too large, or you run the risk of having your entire meal dumped on the ground because you pushed all the veggies and meat to one side to reheat the pasta. Hint: if you are using a larger pan, metal tent stakes make a good ad hoc cooking rack. Use Lexan® or wood utensils to reduce the chances of scratching the pan's surface. Need a lid? Fold a section of foil. Works great with a pot, too.

Pots come in all sizes and shapes, although most individuals will never need more than a one-quart pot for the cooking they do. Make sure that the handle is sturdy and well-attached. One old faithful is a standard one-quart pot with a wide, bail-type handle from a Mirro cook kit. If you don't worry too much about aluminum and Alzheimer's, this bit of hardware will keep you munching for years. If you plan to sauté in the pot before adding liquids, you may want to consider switching to a non-stick pot so you cook with less fat. Clean-up is easier, too.

There are always going to be recipes that are exceptions to the no-stick idea—dishes that just demand a bit of oil, if only for flavoring. But, in general, using a coated pot or pan makes good lite cooking sense.

Ovens are a bit more esoteric. There is really just one backpack oven available at this time that's been designed to cook main courses in a fashion similar to the way you'd cook in a kitchen...The Outback Oven®. There are some rather ancient Mirro ovens still floating around that use boiling water to cook baked goods. And the modern BakePacker® works on a similar principle. Coleman does make a huge fold-up box that fits on top of the multi-burner stoves, but it's not portable unless you are a yak.

The Outback Oven opens a wide range of possibilities for cooking within certain limitations.

The oven in your kitchen operates on the convection principle. Heating elements bring the air in the bottom of the oven to a particular temperature. That air rises on a convection current in the oven, heating foods or cooking vessels holding food and in the process cooking the food.

The Outback Oven sits on top of a one-burner stove, using a reflective heat-resistant cloth tent as the body of the oven, capturing the heat. The top and bottom pan of the oven itself are like a baking dish you'd use in a regular oven. This arrangement works great for casseroles, pizzas and other covered dishes. But, if you want to bake a potato or sear a roast, you'll have to try something else.

You could make your own convection oven. It's not that complicated and has been described elsewhere. The results are very tasty for those adventurous enough to try.

Scraping On By

If the front end of a meal is fun and games, the back end is work. Clean-up is a necessary part of any cooking experience. And that's a great reason to use just one pan!

Here's all it takes. After you eat, scrape the pot or pan (or oven dish) clean with a plastic or wooden spoon or spatula. Don't toss those calories away. Eat them! Besides attracting unwanted visitors late at night, that food you're pitching is still good. Waste not...

Pour water into the pan and relight your stove. Heat the water and add a few drops of dish soap (many biodegradable soaps are available). Add a dash of cold water and scrub to remove all remaining food particles. Dump the water well away from your campsite and at least 100 feet from any water supply.

In your cook kit, you should always pack a few ounces of chlorine bleach along with your scrub pad and towel. The bleach supplies that margin of safety between a not-so-attentive cleaning job and the galloping crud.

Put some more water in the pan and heat to boiling. Add a few drops of bleach to sterilize completely and dispose of the water in the same manner as before. Air dry your pot or pan. Now relax and have a cup of something hot.

THE NON-STICK SKILLET

Had enough of the hows and whys? Let's get ready to do some serious eating...and when we mean serious, remember we're talking about keeping the furnace stoked without putting fat into the fire.

All recipes (except for those noted) are for a single camper. Cooking for two? Double up the portions with an added pinch for good measure. If you're going to cook for larger parties, you may not need to triple or quadruple main ingredients. You'll make up food bulk in side dishes. Just remember the old outdoor chef's rule: Many cooks not needed...Many backs and backpacks are.

Breakfast In The Skillet

In the old days, a few slices of bacon popping in a skillet over a roaring fire meant breakfast was well on its way. Then, nutritional scientists studied our much loved bacon. What did they learn?

First, that sodium nitrates and sodium nitrites are cancer-causing devils.

Then they looked at the fat. A pound of bacon yields slightly more than a quarter pound of edible food. That contains 63 grams of fat (of which 22 are saturated fat). An amazing 77% of bacon's calories come from fat.

Not enough bad news? Those 4.5 ounces of cooked bacon contain over 2,000 milligrams of sodium...400 short of the recommended daily intake. Not exactly the way Mother Nature intended to send us off on a healthy hike or a day of canoeing.

Breakfast on the trail is the most important meal of the day. It should start us off right and keep us going throughout the morning. So what can you do? Try one of the following healthy recipes.

Healthy Eggs

If we can't have bacon sizzling in the skillet, then eggs make a dandy alternative. Try some of the new no-fat egg substitutes, like Egg Beaters® or Second Nature™. They look, taste and act like the real deal, minus the fat and cholesterol of the original vein-cloggers. Biggest plus for no-fat egg substitutes? They come frozen, so you can pack them and they'll be defrosted when you need them. They are also pasteurized, so there should be no problem with nasty bacteria that can come along for the ride with fresh, real eggs.

Low-Fat Scrambled Eggs

1 (8-ounce) container, defrosted Egg-Beaters® or other nonfat egg substitute
3 tablespoons skim milk (use instant if you want)
salt and pepper to taste
1 teaspoon canola oil

Combine the non-fat egg substitute, milk, salt and pepper in a bowl and beat until well mixed. Preheat non-stick skillet and add oil. Pour eggs into skillet and let cook undisturbed for about 30 seconds. At this point, add "extras" (see below) and stir in with spatula, scraping bottom of skillet as you continue to turn the eggs until done.

Suggestion: Round out the meal with a hard roll, fruit and a beverage.

Nutritional information per serving: 176 calories (23.5% from fat), 4.6 g. fat, 0.4 g. protein, 6.2 g. carbohydrates, 1 mg. cholesterol.

Scrambled Egg Extras

Add any of the following to the recipe above for variety.

Meat: 98% fat-free ham, diced; sliced fat-free hot dog; shredded fat-free baloney; cooked chicken breast; chunks of water-packed tuna; slices of low-fat smoked sausage.

Cheese: Any fat-reduced cheese; cubes of non-fat cream cheese.

Spices: diced oregano, basil or dill; Tabasco sauce.

Fire up your morning eggs by adding dried mushrooms, parsley, onions or green peppers, or get a little wild with some dried fruits like apricots, raisins or cranberries.

Green Eggs, No Ham...Ma'am

2 teaspoons canola oil
2 medium potatoes, chopped
¼ cup chopped green pepper
1 small sweet onion, chopped
salt and pepper to taste
½ (8-ounce) carton nonfat egg substitute

¼ **cup shredded nonfat sharp cheese**
¼ **cup bread crumbs**

Preheat a non-stick skillet. Add the oil and then the potatoes. Cook three to four minutes, flipping with wooden or plastic spatula. Add green pepper and onion. Continue cooking until potatoes start to brown. Add salt and pepper.

Lower the flame and pour the egg substitute over all. Cover skillet and cook until eggs are done. Cover with cheese and bread crumbs. Serve.

Nutritional information per serving: 516 calories (18.8% from fat), 10.8 g. fat., 26 g. protein, 76.5 g. carbohydrates, no cholesterol.

Let's take a "cook's" tour with three tasty egg messes.

East Side Eggers

1 teaspoon olive oil
¼ **pound low-fat smoked sausage, sliced thin**
1 (8-ounce) container nonfat egg substitute
garlic powder to taste
salt and pepper to taste

Preheat non-stick skillet over medium flame and add olive oil. Add smoked sausage and cook slowly. Turn once so that each side is crispy.

Lower the flame slightly and pour egg substitute over smoked sausage. Season with garlic powder, salt and pepper. Cook slowly, like an omelette, until the bottom of the eggs are browned to a golden hue and top is firm (three to four minutes, depending on heat). Slide out of skillet onto plate and flip back into skillet to cook top, taking care not to burn.

Nutritional information per serving: 300 calories (23% from fat), 7.7 g. fat, 42 g. protein, 5 g. carbohydrates, 50 mgs. cholesterol.

If you feel like Lorenzo, then you'll enjoy being served...

Machiavelli's Eye Openers

1 teaspoon olive oil
1 small onion, diced
1 teaspoon salt
¼ **teaspoon black pepper**
2 small tomatoes, cored and chopped
1 cup freeze-dried peas, rehydrated

½ cup water
1 (8-ounce) carton nonfat egg substitute
3 tablespoons grated Parmesan cheese

Preheat non-stick skillet over medium flame and add olive oil. When oil is hot, sauté onions. Add salt, pepper and tomatoes and cook uncovered over low flame for about 20 minutes, stirring occasionally.

Add peas and water and cook another ten minutes. Carefully pour egg substitute, a quarter-cup at a time, as for poaching. Continue to cook over low flame for another 20 minutes without stirring. Sprinkle with the Parmesan cheese. Serve.

Suggestion: About ten minutes before serving, you may gently add a couple of chunks of French/Italian bread into the egg/sauce mixture to soak up a bit of the sauce and thicken things.

Nutritional information per serving: 390 calories (16% from fat), 7 g. fat, 36 g. protein, 46 g. carbohydrates, 4 mgs. cholesterol.

A sizzling way to get your morning started.

Yucatan Scramble

2 fat-free flour tortillas
1 teaspoon canola oil
1 (8-ounce) container nonfat egg substitute
1 dash Tabasco sauce
1 cup canned pinto beans, drained
1 tablespoon black olives, diced
2 ounces reduced-fat Muenster cheese, shredded
bottled salsa, if desired

Heat a non-stick skillet over a medium flame. Add tortillas, one at a time and cook until warmed through. When each tortilla is warm, remove and set aside, covered.

Return skillet to flame. Add canola oil, and when hot add the egg substitute and Tabasco sauce. Scramble eggs. About halfway through the scrambling, add the pinto beans. Once done, remove from flame and stir in cheese and olives. Roll in tortillas and top with salsa. Serves two.

Nutritional information per serving: 408 calories (18% from fat), 8.2 g. fat, 33 g. protein, 50.3 g. carbohydrates, no cholesterol.

Omelettes

Omelettes are like scrambled eggs, except lighter. You can customize an omelette any way you wish.

The Omelette From Two Don Street

1 (8-ounce) container nonfat egg substitute
1 tablespoon water
1 teaspoon canola oil

Add the container of nonfat egg substitute and water to a mixing bowl. With a fork, beat until froth begins to build.

Over a medium flame, preheat small non-stick skillet and add oil. Pour omelette mixture into skillet slowly, allowing eggs to spread evenly across the bottom of the skillet. Rotate skillet gently to build a lip around the edge of the egg. Cook slowly until top of eggs is firm and bottom is browned lightly.

At this point, add meat, cheese, veggie or whatever to one half of the omelette...say from 12 o'clock to 6 o'clock, with the skillet handle at 9 o'clock. Gently slide your plastic spatula under the edge of the egg all the way around to separate from the skillet. Finish with the portion opposite the skillet handle. Lift egg with spatula as you tip the skillet and slide egg out onto plate. When the egg is half on the plate (and half in the skillet) flip the remaining half over to close omelette. The heat of the egg will melt cheese and heat meat and veggies.

Nutritional information per serving (plain): 160 calories (25% from fat), 4.5 g. fat, 24 g. protein, 4 g. carbohydrates, no cholesterol.

Somewhere, there is a Dublin-Nuevo Laredo connection. There are at least two super Mexican restaurants in the nation that have more than a little of the Irish flowing.

Carlos O'Rourke's Hat Dance

1 teaspoon olive oil
½ medium unpeeled potato, sliced
½ medium onion, chopped
2 tablespoons pimento-stuffed olives, sliced
ground black pepper to taste
1 (8-ounce) carton nonfat egg substitute

Over a medium flame, heat a non-stick skillet. Add olive oil. When the oil is hot, add the potatoes and onions and cook until tender.

Remove the potatoes and onions from the skillet with slotted spoon and place on plate. Add olives and pepper to carton of egg substitute and shake until combined. Reduce the flame to low and pour egg mixture into the skillet, tipping the skillet to evenly spread the egg out to the edge. Every once in a while, run the spatula around the edges of the egg to loosen from the skillet. When partially cooked through, add onion and potato and fold omelette. Cook until egg is firm. Then slide onto plate.

Nutritional information per serving: 284 calories (20% from fat), 6.3 g. fat, 26 g. protein, 29 g. carbohydrates, no cholesterol.

This recipe is an easy way to combine scrambled eggs and maple syrup, and a *bon, bon* way to start your day.

Parisian Sunrise

½ cup nonfat egg substitute
3 slices of slightly stale bread
1 teaspoon canola oil
maple syrup, jelly or powdered sugar

Pour egg substitute into plate or flat skillet. Add bread slices and allow to soak until thoroughly moist.

While bread is soaking, over medium-low flame begin heating the non-stick skillet. Add the canola oil, and when hot place one or two slices (depending on skillet size) into the skillet to cook. Allow to brown well before flipping. Remove to plate and serve with favorite topping.

Nutritional information per serving (without topping): 295 calories (22.8% from fat), 7.5 g. fat, 0.9 g. protein, 39.2 g. carbohydrates, no cholesterol.

Pancakes Etc.

Too much cluck can make you a bit crazy on the trail. There are meals of legendary proportions...you know, sort of Paul Bunyan-esque...that are built around one of the easiest dishes you can make: the humble pancake.

Dry Sack Cakes

Mix these dry ingredients at home and place in resealable plastic bag:

1 cup all-purpose flour (not self-rising)
1 teaspoon white or yellow corn meal
1 teaspoon granulated brown sugar
¾ teaspoon baking soda
1 teaspoon baking powder

At campsite, add the following:

¼ cup nonfat egg substitute
1 cup skim milk (use powdered with equivalent water)
canola oil

Mix the dry and wet ingredients together in a bowl until blended but still lumpy. Over a medium flame, begin heating the non-stick skillet and with a paper towel, rub a bit of canola oil onto the skillet. Pour a half-cup of the batter into the skillet, tipping to spread batter out slightly. Cook until bubbles appear in the center of the pancake and the edges begin to appear dry. Flip pancake and cook until steam stops coming from pancake. Remove cooked pancake, keep covered while beginning the process again, until batter is used up. Serve. Makes four pancakes.

Nutritional information per serving: 591 calories (4% from fat), 2.7 g. fat, 26 g. protein, 111.6 g. carbohydrates, 4 mgs. cholesterol.

You can get fruity with pancakes by adding just about anything from berries to bananas.

Dutchman's Griddle

2 tablespoons reduced-fat margarine
2 apples, peeled, cored and sliced
¼ cup maple syrup
¾ cup low-fat Bisquick® mix
1 cup skim milk (use powdered with equivalent water)
¼ cup nonfat egg substitute
1½ teaspoons canola oil
¼ teaspoon ground cinnamon
¼ teaspoon grated nutmeg

To a non-stick skillet, placed over a medium flame, add the margarine and apples. When they begin to sizzle, add the maple syrup and cook until the apples are tender. Remove from the flame and set aside.

In a bowl, stir the Bisquick® with the skim milk, egg substitute, oil, cinnamon and nutmeg until it forms a batter; it should appear slightly lumpy. Remove the apples from the skillet with a slotted spoon and reserve the liquid. Add the apples to the batter and stir until just combined.

Place the skillet over a medium flame. When hot, wipe bottom and sides with canola oil. Pour batter with apples into the skillet. Turn once and cook until golden brown. Serve with syrup for great meal for two.

Nutritional information per serving: 651 calories (12.7% from fat), 9.2 g. fat, 29 g. protein, 114 g. carbohydrates, 12 mgs. cholesterol.

Healthy Lunch and Dinner

We'll divide things up by protein source, starting with poultry since it is so low in fat.

Poultry

To keep fat content as low as possible, it is important to always use the white meat, whether it comes from chicken, turkey or game hen.

Breast meat is the leanest on the bird. Removing the skin removes the fattest part. A split skinless chicken breast has only three grams of fat.

We suggest you buy your chicken fresh. According to the federal government, that means the bird should not have been cooled below 26° F.

There is an aesthetic reason for buying fresh. One less freezing and thawing has a good effect on the flavor and texture of the meat. Then, there is a practical reason. Most stores don't package frozen poultry in single-serving sizes. You have to defrost the chicken to repackage it, and then refreeze it. Not a good idea for tasty, tender eating.

Buy your poultry already skinned and boned. That will save you considerable effort and you won't have to figure out what to with the bones at the campsite. (Some scavengers don't realize the damage those bones may cause them.)

Crossing the International Dateline is a great way to start our culinary tour. East Asia is not a red-meat-rich area...but poultry...now that's a different story!

Snowy Chicken

1 whole chicken breast, skinned, boned and cut into one-inch pieces
¼ cup cornstarch
1 egg white (*see note)
2 tablespoons white wine
2 teaspoons peanut oil, divided

4 mushrooms, sliced
4 ounces fresh snow peas, strings removed
¼ teaspoon ground ginger
¼ cup watercress or spinach leaves
salt and pepper to taste

Dust the chicken with cornstarch. Set aside. In a bowl, combine the egg white and wine, beating well.

Add one teaspoon of the oil to the non-stick skillet and place over a medium flame. When hot, add the mushrooms; stir and cook until they begin to give up some liquid. Add the snow peas and ginger to the skillet and cook for two minutes, stirring frequently. Remove all from skillet with slotted spoon and place on plate.

Place egg mixture and chicken in bowl. Set aside. Add remaining oil to skillet and when hot, add chicken with liquid to skillet and cook for two minutes. Add peas and mushrooms and watercress or spinach and cook until all is done, about three or four more minutes. Serve with rice.

*Note: Separate egg white from yolk by carefully breaking egg in half and passing yolk and white from side to side in shells until yolk is on one side and the bulk of the white is on the other.

Suggestion: Minute Rice® or other quick-cooking rice products are a big boon to outdoor cooking. The package is light enough to pack in, and the food cooks up in no time. A great bargain.

Nutritional information per serving: 567 calories (19.8% from fat), 12.5 g. fat, 61 g. protein, 42 g. carbohydrates, 136 mgs. cholesterol.

Cash Chew Chicken

2 teaspoons peanut oil
1 whole chicken breast, split, boned, and skinned, cut into one-inch pieces
½ cup orange juice
½ teaspoon ground ginger
½ teaspoon salt
½ cup raisins
1 (6-ounce) can water chestnuts
½ cup white wine
1 tablespoon salted cashews
1 tablespoon cornstarch, mixed in two tablespoons water
1 cup cooked white rice

Add oil to the non-stick skillet and place over a medium flame. When

hot, add the chicken pieces and lightly brown, about four to five minutes. Add the orange juice, ginger, salt, raisins, water chestnuts and
wine. Bring to a simmer, reduce the flame to low and simmer for 20
minutes. Add the cashews and the cornstarch mixture, stirring until the
sauce is thick. Serve over the rice. Serves two.

Nutritional information per serving: *529 calories (15.5% from fat), 9.1 g. fat,
32 g. protein, 74 g. carbohydrates, 68 mgs. cholesterol.*

Moving westward around the globe, we come to India. Bengali cuisine is a mixture of tasty vegetables and exotic spices—perfect for
a special evening trail banquet.

Delhi-icious Chicken

   2 teaspoons canola oil
   1 medium onion, chopped
   1 whole chicken breast, split, boned, skinned and cut into 1- inch
      cubes
   1 tablespoon all-purpose flour
   1 tablespoon hot curry powder (or to taste)
   ¼ teaspoon ground ginger
   2 tablespoons honey
   2 tablespoons sodium-reduced soy sauce
   2 reduced-sodium chicken bouillon cubes
   2 cups water
   ¾ cup uncooked long-grain white rice
   1 large carrot, peeled and sliced

Place non-stick skillet over medium flame and add the oil and onions.
Sauté until onions are browned (about six minutes). Add chicken and
brown. Sprinkle the flour, curry and ginger into skillet and stir. Add the
honey, soy sauce, bouillon cubes and water. Stir until bouillon cubes
dissolve. Lower flame and simmer five minutes. Add the rice and carrot.
Simmer uncovered for 20 minutes, stirring occasionally. Serves two.

Nutritional information per serving: *581 calories (11% from fat), 7.1 g. fat,
35.5 g. protein, 91 g. carbohydrates, 69 mgs. cholesterol.*

Curry and ginger together can make a taste bud bonfire. A little
sweeter taste is attained by losing the ginger and adding some cit-
rus and honey, as in this colorful dish.

Madras Poulet

1 whole chicken breast, split, boned and skinned, cut into one-inch cubes
¼ cup sodium-reduced soy sauce
2 tablespoons lime juice
1 teaspoon honey
¼ teaspoon hot curry powder
1 medium green pepper, chopped
1 medium red pepper, chopped
½ cup bean sprouts, chopped
1 teaspoon canola oil

In a bowl, stir together all the ingredients except the oil. Marinate for 20 minutes. Heat the non-stick skillet over a high flame until hot (To test, drip a bead of water into skillet; it should dance) and add the oil.

Drain off the marinade and add the mixture to the skillet. Stir-fry for about five minutes or until veggies are tender. Pour the marinade over all and bring to a boil, simmer for one minute. Serve.

Nutritional information per serving: 426 calories (16.6% from fat), 7.9 g. fat, 65 g. protein, 27.4 g. carbohydrates, 136 mgs. cholesterol.

Chicken Scallopini is great served over spaghetti. To save time and pans, precook the spaghetti at home and store in an air-tight plastic container. Then, just add to the mix when cooking is complete.

Chicken Scallopini

¼ cup all-purpose flour
½ teaspoon salt
¼ teaspoon black pepper
¼ cup nonfat egg substitute
1 chicken breast, skinned, boned and cut into one-inch cubes
2 teaspoons olive oil
1 garlic clove, peeled and sliced
1 reduced-sodium chicken bouillon cube
¾ cup boiling water
¼ cup dry red wine
4 mushrooms, sliced
1 to 1½ cups precooked spaghetti or pasta

Add the flour, salt and pepper to a reclosable plastic bag. Add the egg substitute to a bowl. Dip the chicken into eggs and then place in the bag with the flour mixture; shaking until well-coated.

Place the non-stick skillet over a medium flame. Add the oil and garlic and sauté until the garlic begins to brown. Lower the flame, add the chicken and sauté until brown. Add the bouillon cube, water, wine and mushrooms. Simmer uncovered for 15 minutes. Add pasta and heat.

Notes: If you wish to take the high-but-just-as-lean road with a more traditional approach, you can substitute veal cutlets for the chicken.

If garlic is too much for you, try using fresh basil leaves. Simply substitute the basil for the garlic and sauté in the oil until the leaves just wilt. Do not brown. Gives a unique, lighter flavor.

Nutritional information per serving: 755 calories (16.5% from fat), 13.9 g. fat, 70 g. protein, 70 g. carbohydrates, 70 mgs. cholesterol.

Another traditional chicken dish that has brightened the serving board of many a red-sauce region household is also one of those "Gee, I never knew it was good for me" Italian dishes.

Catch-As-Catch-Can Chicken

    salt and pepper to taste
    ½ teaspoon garlic powder
    ½ pound white-meat chicken pieces, skin and all visible fat
       removed
    2 teaspoons olive oil
    1 medium onion, sliced
    1 medium green pepper, seeded and sliced
    1 (6-ounce) can tomato paste
    1 cup water
    4 to 6 fresh mushrooms, sliced
    ¼ teaspoon dried oregano, crumbled
    1½ cups precooked spaghetti or linguine

Lightly sprinkle the salt, pepper and garlic powder onto the chicken pieces. Heat the oil in the non-stick skillet over a medium flame. When hot, add the chicken pieces and sauté until lightly browned. Remove the chicken. Add the onion and green pepper to the skillet and sauté until softened, about three to four minutes. Add the tomato paste, water, mushrooms and oregano, stirring until mixed. Return the chicken to the skillet, cover and cook for 20 minutes over a low flame, stirring occasionally. Add the pasta and heat through. Serves two.

Nutritional information per serving: 447 calories (15.7% from fat), 7.8 g. fat, 35 g. protein, 58 g. carbohydrates, 68 mgs. cholesterol.

Eastern European countries have delicious ways with chicken, too. Sweet paprika, onions and peppers are usually featured.

Also used in abundance are high-fat dairy products, like sour cream. A cup of sour cream contains 50 fat grams, with plenty of saturated fat coming along for the ride. The following recipe is a low-fat re-creation of a classic Hungarian dish.

Chicken Paprika

1 whole chicken breast, split, skinned, and boned
¼ teaspoon black pepper
¼ teaspoon garlic powder
1 teaspoon olive oil
1 medium onion, sliced thin
1 medium green pepper, cut in strips
1 medium tomato, chopped
2 reduced-sodium, chicken bouillon cubes
1 cup water
1 tablespoon sweet Hungarian paprika
1½ cups precooked medium egg noodles

Sprinkle the chicken with the pepper and garlic powder. Add the oil to a non-stick skillet and place over a medium flame. Brown the breasts on both sides. Add the onion and green pepper and cook for two or three minutes. While stirring, add the tomato, bouillon cubes and water. Bring to boil. Add paprika and stir. Reduce flame to low, cover skillet and simmer for ten minutes. Just before serving, stir in egg noodles and simmer for one minute.

Nutritional information per serving: 801 calories (19.3% from fat), 17.2 g. fat, 69 g. protein, 91 g. carbohydrates, 215 mgs. cholesterol.

Vegetables and fruits have their own pecking order when it comes to hitting the trail. Apples are great. Hey, they come with their own packaging and everything is completely biodegradable. Same with potatoes. Ain't Mother Nature great?

Down East Cortland Chicken

1 teaspoon canola oil
1 Cornish game hen, quartered and skinned
salt and pepper to taste
½ teaspoon garlic powder
1 small onion, chopped

¼ cup dry white wine
4 small new potatoes, washed and halved
1 medium apple (Macintosh, Granny Smith or other firm and tart
   apple), cored and chopped

Add the oil to the non-stick skillet and place over a medium flame. Lightly brown the hen quarters on both sides. Sprinkle salt, pepper and garlic powder onto the hen. Add the onion, wine and potatoes to the skillet, stir together, cover, lower the flame and simmer for ten minutes. Stir in the apple; cover the skillet and simmer ten minutes or until the apples are quite soft.

Nutritional information per serving: 590 calories (18% from fat), 11.9 g. fat, 54 g. protein, 53 g. carbohydrates, 166 mgs. cholesterol.

DJ used to pack real butter as opposed to various oils. It wasn't for lubrication, mind you, but rather for its great tasting butterfat content in making a white sauce.

The problem was, the two tablespoons of butter used in the sauce brought with it 25 grams of highly saturated fat. Not exactly the healthiest way to thicken a sauce.

DM created a super way to thicken any sauce and cut out the butter entirely. Cornstarch, swirled into skim milk, works like a charm and adds no fat. Genius at work, here. (Modest, too...wink.)

Lite 'n Saucy Chicken

New White Sauce
   2 tablespoons cornstarch
   1 cup skim milk (made from instant)
For the chicken
   1 whole chicken breast, split, boned and skinned
   1 teaspoon salt
   ¼ teaspoon white pepper
   2 teaspoons olive oil
   ½ cup dry white wine
   1 medium green pepper, cut in strips
   ¾ cup new white sauce

In a cup, stir the cornstarch into the milk until dissolved. Set aside.

Rub the chicken with the salt and pepper. Add the oil to the non-stick skillet and place over a medium flame. Add the chicken to the skillet and sauté until lightly browned, four to five minutes. Add the wine, reduce the flame to low and simmer for 20 minutes. Add the green pepper and sauté for two to three minutes. Add new white sauce and cook until sauce comes to a boil. Serve immediately over bread, rice or couscous.

Nutritional information per serving (without bread, rice or couscous): 471 calories (6.5% from fat), 3.4 g. fat, 61 g. protein, 25.7 g. carbohydrates, 139 mgs. cholesterol.

We've all suffered through rubbery, high-in-fat Chicken a la King. Here's a terrific recipe for that old standby that not only is low in fat but tastes great (filling, too, but less so).

Chicken a la King Lite

4 tablespoons water
½ chicken breast, boned, skinned and diced
¼ teaspoon salt
black pepper to taste
1 teaspoon canola oil
1 small green pepper, chopped
3 mushrooms, cleaned and sliced
2 tablespoons cornstarch
1 tablespoon nonfat egg substitute
¼ teaspoon salt
1 cup skim milk (made from powdered)

Add the water and chicken to the non-stick skillet and place over a medium flame. When the water begins to simmer, reduce the flame to low, cover and cook for four to five minutes, shaking the skillet occasionally. Remove the chicken to a dish and dispose of the water.

Set the flame to medium, return the skillet to the flame and add the oil. When hot, add the green peppers and mushrooms and sauté until softened. Add the chicken and sauté for one minute.

Stir the cornstarch, egg substitute and salt into the milk. When thoroughly combined pour into skillet. Cook until thick, stirring constantly. Simmer for one minute, stirring to avoid scorching. Serve over bread or cooked rice.

Nutritional information per serving (without bread or rice): 358 calories (17% from fat), 6.8 g. fat, 37 g. protein, 33.6 g. carbohydrates, 72 mgs. cholesterol.

The sweet taste of basil is one of our favorites and plays a big role in our outback spice rack.

Basil's Full Meal Chicken

¼ cup all-purpose flour
½ teaspoon sweet paprika
¼ teaspoon salt
⅛ teaspoon black pepper
1 whole chicken breast, split, skinned and boned
2 teaspoons olive oil
1 green onion, chopped
½ cup sliced green beans
1 chicken bouillon cube
½ cup water
1 large tomato, chopped
½ teaspoon dried basil leaves, crumbled
1 cup precooked pasta
1 tablespoon grated Parmesan cheese

Combine the flour, paprika, salt and pepper in a bowl. Dredge the chicken in the flour mixture. Add the oil to the non-stick skillet and place over a medium flame. Cook the chicken until lightly browned, about four to five minutes, turning frequently. Add the onions and beans and sauté for one to two minutes. Add the bouillon cube, water, tomatoes, and basil and simmer uncovered for five minutes. Stir in the pasta, cook until heated through, about one minute. Dust with the Parmesan cheese. Serve.

Nutritional information per serving: 720 calories (19.6% from fat), 15.7 g. fat, 67 g. protein, 73 g. carbohydrates, 141 mgs. cholesterol.

Vegetables

Studies show we are eating more vegetables than ever before. Very healthy and very low in fat, they also are a tremendous natural source for the vitamins, minerals and fiber necessary to keep us fit.

For lite campsite eating, it's not necessary to become a complete vegetarian. As a change of focus, rethink your main dish from time-to-time, and build it around something green...or orange...or even purple.

Veggies give our palates a whole new perspective. Another neat thing about vegetables is that they are usually prepackaged by Mother Nature and don't require a lot of refrigeration. But, vegetables bruise easily; take good care of them and they will return the f(l)avor.

Ragout, like ratatouille, is European for "What's in the fridge?"

Easy-Does-It Eggplant Ragout

1 teaspoon olive oil
1 small onion, chopped
1 small green pepper, chopped
1 small eggplant, sliced julienne-style
1 medium tomato, chopped
1 (6-ounce) can tomato paste
½ cup water
salt and pepper to taste
¼ teaspoon sweet paprika
¼ teaspoon dried basil leaves, crumbled

Add the oil to the non-stick skillet and place over a medium flame. Add the onion and sauté for two minutes. Add the green pepper and sauté for one minute. Add the eggplant, and tomato and sauté for three minutes. Add the tomato paste and when it begins to bubble add the water, salt, pepper, paprika and basil. Set the flame to low and simmer, uncovered for 15 minutes, stirring occasionally.

Suggestion: When the ragout is finished, set aside and prepare instant rice. Serve the ragout over the rice and dust with Parmesan cheese.

Nutritional information per serving: 297 calories (20% from fat), 6.6 g. fat, 7 g. protein, 58.4 g. carbohydrates, no cholesterol.

Side dishes spice up any meal. Actually, a veggie or two on the side is not unusual. Vegetables cook very nicely in a non-stick skillet. And, the potato is a carbo-loaded veggie that travels well.

Belly-Warmer Hash Browns

1 large baking potato, baked ahead, cooled, placed in a sealed
   container and refrigerated
1-½ teaspoons olive oil
1 medium onion, chopped
salt and pepper to taste
2 slices 98% fat-free smoked ham, torn or chopped

Slice the unpeeled potato thinly. Add the oil to the non-stick skillet and place over a medium flame. Add the onions and sauté until tender, but not crisp, about four to five minutes. Add the potatoes and continue cooking until the potatoes begin to brown. Add the salt, pepper and ham and sauté for one to two minutes. Serve.

Nutritional information per serving: 365 calories (18.4% from fat), 7.5 g. fat, 8 g. protein, 66 g. carbohydrates, 8 mgs. cholesterol.

Zesty Fast Fries

2 large baking potato, baked ahead, cooled, placed in a sealed container and refrigerated
1 tablespoon olive oil
1 tablespoon Tabasco sauce
seasoned salt (optional)

Cut the potatoes into quarter-inch spears. Place the potatoes and Tabasco sauce in plastic bag and shake to coat.

Add the oil to the non-stick skillet and place over a medium flame. When the oil is hot (a drop of water sizzles when carefully dropped on the skillet) add the potatoes and cook for three to five minutes, stirring occasionally so they will brown evenly on all sides. Sprinkle with the optional seasoned salt. Sizzlin'...yes!

Nutritional information per serving: 559 calories (21.8% from fat), 13.6 g. fat, 10 g. protein, 105 g. carbohydrates, no cholesterol.

Now, if you want to really spice things up...

"Ya, Hey Dare"-Style Mountain Fries

½ pound baking potatoes, baked ahead, diced
2 teaspoons olive oil
1 small onion, sliced thin
4 ounces low-fat smoked sausage
½ teaspoon garlic powder
¾ teaspoon ground cumin
1 teaspoon marjoram leaves, crumbled
salt and black pepper to taste
1 tablespoon finely chopped fresh parsley leaves

Add the oil to the non-stick skillet and place over a medium flame. When hot, add the onion and sauté for five minutes, until soft. Add potatoes and sausage and sauté for ten minutes or until golden brown. Stir in the garlic powder, cumin, marjoram, salt and pepper. Continue to sauté one minute more. Dust with the parsley. Serve.

Nutritional information per serving: 526 calories (21.9% from fat), 12.8 g. fat, 24 g. protein, 71 g. carbohydrates, 50 mgs. cholesterol.

Spuds 'n Peppers

    2 teaspoons olive oil
    2 medium potatoes (russets are perfect), peeled and sliced thin
    I small green pepper, cored and sliced thin
    I small red pepper, cored and sliced thin
    ¼ teaspoon cayenne pepper (or to taste)
    salt and pepper to taste
    garlic powder to taste

Add the oil to the non-stick skillet and place over a medium flame. When hot, add the potatoes to the skillet. Cook, stirring, for four to five minutes. Add the peppers and continue cooking until the potatoes are browned and crispy. Add the seasonings. Serve.

Suggestion: To make a complete, yet lite meal of this, push the vegetables to the side of the skillet and cook a boneless, skinless breast of chicken in the juices for about ten minutes, flipping occasionally.

Nutritional information per serving: 448 calories (18.8% from fat), 9.4 g. fat, 10 g. protein, 86 g. carbohydrates, no cholesterol.

Mushrooms are a viable source of protein. You need about two cups of sliced mushrooms to replace a three-ounce serving of meat. The recipe doesn't quite make that mark, but it's a great combination of favorite flavors.

Hamish MacShrooms

    2 teaspoons cornstarch
    ½ cup skim milk (made from powdered)
    1 teaspoon olive oil
    3 mushrooms, diced
    1 small onion, diced
    1 cup pre-cooked macaroni
    4 ounces 98% fat-free baked ham, chopped
    2 tablespoons grated Parmesan cheese

In a cup, stir together the cornstarch and milk. Set aside. Add the oil to the non-stick skillet and place over a medium flame. When hot, add the mushrooms and onions and sauté until tender, but not brown. Add the milk mixture, macaroni, ham and cheese and toss over low flame for a minute or two until the sauce thickens and the macaroni is hot. Serve.

Nutritional information per serving: 545 calories (22.2% from fat), 13.5 g. fat, 36 g. protein, 64.3 g. carbohydrates, 62 mgs. cholesterol.

Shrooms n' Squash

1 teaspoon olive oil
1 medium onion, diced
5 to 6 mushrooms, sliced
1 medium yellow summer squash, diced
¼ teaspoon garlic powder
¼ teaspoon black pepper
salt to taste

Add the oil to the non-stick skillet and place over a medium flame. Add the onion and sauté until tender, about four to five minutes. Add the mushrooms and sauté for three minutes. Add the squash, garlic powder, black pepper and salt. Continue cooking until squash reaches desired tenderness. Crisp-tender (preferred) will take only two or three minutes.

Nutritional information per serving: 172 calories (27.7% from fat), 5.3 g. fat, 3 g. protein, 27.9 g. carbohydrates, no cholesterol.

If there is a shortcoming with vegetables, it's that they may take a long time to cook. There is one foolproof method to get around the veggie cook time roadblock, and that's by blanching them before cooking. Blanching works best with firm vegetables such as green beans, broccoli, carrots or cauliflower. It's a short process, something you can do at home before you hit the road.

Here's how: Fill a medium bowl with cold water and ice. Set aside. Bring about two cups of water (or enough to cover vegetables completely) to a boil in a pot. Place selected vegetables in the water and cook for exactly two minutes. Remove with a slotted spoon and dunk in ice water. This stops the cooking instantly and chills everything immediately. Drain and place in a resealable plastic bag. Refrigerate until needed.

Now, what to use those blanched vegetables in? Try this.

Nuts to you Green Beans

½ teaspoon olive oil
2 teaspoons almonds, sliced
1½ cups green beans, cut to one-inch pieces, blanched and
** packed in plastic bag**

Add the oil to the non-stick skillet and place over a low flame. Add the almonds and sauté gently (taking care not to burn them) until lightly browned. Add the beans and increase the heat to a medium flame. Toss the beans and almonds together for about a minute—long enough for the beans to heat, but not long enough for the almonds to burn.

Suggestion: Try this with broccoli florets for a delicious spin on a much-maligned vegetable.

Nutritional information per serving: 87 calories (41% from fat), 4 g. fat, 0.4 g. protein, 12.2 g. carbohydrates, no cholesterol.

Flying Vegetables

2 teaspoons peanut oil
1½ cups mixed vegetables (green beans, broccoli or cauliflower florets, diced carrots, diced onions, mushrooms, green and/or red peppers, pea pods)
1 tablespoon sodium-reduced soy sauce
¼ teaspoon garlic powder (or to taste)
¼ teaspoon ground ginger (or to taste)
ground black pepper to taste
1 cup precooked white rice

Place the non-stick skillet over a high flame and add the oil. When hot (it won't take long), add the onions and cook for 30 seconds. Add the remaining vegetables, except the pea pods. Sauté for 2-3 minutes until bright green and tender. Add the pea pods and sauté for two more minutes. Add the soy sauce, garlic, ginger and pepper. Toss and sauté for another 30 seconds. Pour over precooked rice.

Suggestion: A slice or two of bread is great for sopping up the wonderfully flavored juices left on the plate.

Nutritional information per serving: 317 calories (20.7% from fat), 7.3 g. fat, 9 g. protein, 56 g. carbohydrates, no cholesterol.

An Old World favorite can dress up your New World trek in a very lite way just by making a few minor changes.

Potato Pancakes

¼ cup nonfat egg substitute
1 tablespoon all-purpose flour (not self-rising)
½ teaspoon baking powder
2 potatoes, peeled and grated
2 teaspoons canola oil

In a bowl, stir together the egg substitute, flour and baking powder until well combined. Add the potatoes and stir until coated. Form into flat cakes. Place the non-stick skillet over a medium flame and add the oil. When hot, add the pancakes. Cook like regular pancakes, turning to brown both sides well.

Nutritional information per serving: 468 calories (17.8% from fat), 9.3 g. fat, 15 g. protein, 84 g. carbohydrates, no cholesterol.

Meat

We can only eat so much chicken and turkey before we've gotta have some red meat. There is absolutely no reason not to have some beef or pork—or even buffalo—as a part of an evening meal. However, to keep campsite dining as light in fat as possible it is very important to make certain the meat is properly selected.

When it comes to ground beef, purchase only 90 or 95%-lean meat. A three-ounce patty of 80%-lean ground beef contains 17 grams of fat, with over 70% of its calories coming from fat. Surprised? That same three-ounce patty made from 95%-lean beef has a little more than four grams of fat, with 34% of its calories coming from fat. We call that a big fat difference.

Also, if space in the burger is not being taken up with fat, it is being taken up with protein—the perfect material to help keep muscles strong throughout sometimes grueling outdoor activities. The right selection is a good choice.

If you're new to outdoor cooking, you might want to start out with lean ground beef. You can abuse it and still end up with a reasonable result.

Burger Sling

8 ounces 95%-lean ground beef
½ medium onion, diced
½ cup pinto beans (previously canned and re-packed in a plastic bag)
4 tablespoons tomato ketchup
1 tablespoon brown sugar
½ cup water
1 reduced-sodium beef bouillon cube
salt and pepper to taste
1 cup prepared white rice

Place the non-stick skillet over a medium flame and to it add the ground beef. Cook the beef until it has lost its pink color, breaking up with the edge of a plastic spatula or spoon. Add the onion and cook until tender, about four minutes. Add all the remaining ingredients, except for the rice. Bring to a boil, reduce the flame to low and simmer for ten minutes or until the sauce is smooth and the beans are tender. Serve over the rice.

Nutritional information per serving: 636 calories (17.5% from fat), 12.4 g. fat, 53 g. protein, 76.8 g. carbohydrates, 124 mgs. cholesterol.

Burger Borscht

8 ounces 95%-lean ground beef
1 small onion, minced
¼ cup pickled beets, diced
½ cup cooked potato, diced
¼ teaspoon salt
⅛ teaspoon black pepper
1 teaspoon canola oil

In bowl, gently mix all ingredients except for the canola oil. Add the oil to the non-stick skillet and place over a medium flame. When hot, place the mixture onto the skillet's hot surface and flatten with a spatula to about one-inch thick. Cover and cook for 3-5 minutes or until browned. Flip once, cover and continue cooking for five minutes. Serve.

Suggestion: Serve with hardtack or rye bread.

Nutritional information per serving: 468 calories (30.7% from fat), 16 g. fat, 50 g. protein, 30 g. carbohydrates, 124 mgs. cholesterol.

Smokey Burgers

8 ounces 95%-lean ground beef
½ small onion, chopped
¼ teaspoon Liquid Smoke®
black pepper to taste
garlic powder to taste
1 teaspoon canola oil
2 slices rye bread

Add all the ingredients, except for the oil and bread, to a bowl and knead until just mixed. Take care not to over-mix. Shape the mixture into two half-inch-thick burgers. Add the oil to the non-stick skillet and place over a medium flame. When hot, add the burgers. Cook for five minutes per side for medium. Serve on the sliced rye bread.

Suggestion: If you're a cheeseburger nut, place two slices of non-fat sharp cheese over each burger during the last minute of cooking. By serving these on split Kaiser rolls with a green salad and nonfat dressing, you'll bring the calories from fat for the meal to below 20 percent.

Nutritional information per serving: 501 calories (31.7% from fat), 17.7 g. fat, 52 g. protein, 31 g. carbohydrates, 124 mgs. cholesterol.

Goulash. There have got to be at least 5,000 versions of this dish. The variety is endless. This is DJ's mom's great interpretation.

DJ's Mom's Goulash-Go-Litely

    1 teaspoon canola oil
    ⅓ pound 95%-lean ground beef
    salt and black pepper to taste
    1 medium onion, diced
    1 medium sweet green pepper, diced
    ½ teaspoon dried oregano leaves, crumbled
    ¼ teaspoon garlic powder
    ¼ teaspoon dried basil leaves, crumbled
    ½ teaspoon sugar
    1 medium, fresh tomato, cubed (optional)
    1 (6-ounce) can tomato paste
    1 cup water
    ½ cup precooked elbow macaroni
    1 tablespoon grated Parmesan cheese

Add the oil to the non-stick skillet and place over a medium flame. When hot, add the hamburger and brown, breaking the meat up with the edge of a plastic spatula or spoon. Add the salt, pepper, onion and green pepper and sauté until veggies are soft, about four minutes. Drain off any fat. Return to flame and add remaining ingredients, except for the macaroni and cheese, stirring until tomato paste is dissolved. Simmer for ten minutes. Add macaroni and stir until hot. Serve dusted with the Parmesan cheese.

Suggestion: Crusty French bread goes superbly on the side.

Nutritional information per serving: 615 calories (23.5% from fat), 16.1 g. fat, 45 g. protein, 78.1 g. carbohydrates, 86 mgs. cholesterol.

Meatballs are wonderful, sort of like mini-burgers, each bursting with juice and flavor. Serve with sides of hash browns, or stir-fried green beans, or raw carrots.

M-M-Good Meatballs

8 ounces 95%-lean ground beef
¼ cup seasoned bread crumbs
½ medium onion, chopped fine
salt and pepper to taste
2 teaspoons corn oil
1 cup water
1 (single-serving sized) packet beef-based soup mix

In a bowl, combine the meat with the bread crumbs, onion, salt and pepper. Shape the meat into balls about one to one-and-a-half inches in diameter. Add the oil to the non-stick skillet and place over a medium-low flame. When hot, add the meatballs and brown, rolling them around by tilting the skillet. Add the water and soup mix. Let simmer for five to ten minutes.

Suggestion: To bring the calories from fat down to near 20 percent, add a thin-sliced, unpeeled potato or other vegetables when the broth begins to simmer.

Nutritional information per serving: 498 calories (32% from fat), 17.7 g. fat, 53 g. protein, 30.2 g. carbohydrates, 124 mgs. cholesterol.

Swedish Meatballs

8 ounces 95%-lean ground beef
¼ teaspoon sugar
¼ cup nonfat egg substitute
¼ teaspoon ground sage
¼ teaspoon ground allspice
¼ teaspoon ground nutmeg
1 small onion, chopped fine
1 cup bread crumbs
⅓ cup cold water
2 teaspoons canola oil
1 medium potato, sliced thin
1 small onion, chopped

In a bowl, mix together the ground beef with the sugar, egg substitute, sage, allspice, nutmeg, onion, bread crumbs and water until well combined. (Take care not to over-mix, as over-mixing will toughen the meatballs.) Shape into one-inch meatballs. Add the oil to the non-stick skillet and place over a medium flame. When hot, add the meatballs. Brown evenly by tilting skillet from side to side and rolling meatballs around. Add the potato and onion. Set flame to low, cover with foil and cook for about 20 minutes, periodically shaking the skillet. Serves two.

Hint: When preparing raw meatballs, keep a bowl of cold water by you. Wetting your hands will reduce the chances of the meatballs sticking to your hands.

Nutritional information per serving: 613 calories (19.9% from fat), 13.6 g. fat, 37.5 g. protein, 83 g. carbohydrates, 62 mgs. cholesterol.

Nana's Meatballs

Same as Swedish Meatballs, except substitute one cup instant rice for the bread crumbs. Omit the sage, allspice and nutmeg. Add one-quarter teaspoon each of dried oregano and basil leaves, crumbled.

Ready for something only slightly more challenging than ground beef? The following recipes make great outdoor meals.

If you're hiking during cooler weather, what's better than a pot of chili? This chili will warm you from the inside out.

Lean On Me Chili

   2 teaspoons canola oil
   1 pound top round beef, trimmed of all visible fat and cut into
      half-inch cubes
   1 small onion, chopped
   1 clove garlic, minced
   ½ cup dried corn, rehydrated
   1 (6-ounce) can tomato paste
   1¼ cups water
   2 mild chili peppers, seeded and chopped
   1 teaspoon ground cumin
   ¼ teaspoon salt
   chili powder, to taste
   one or more of the following optional additives: raisins, grapes,
      summer squash, zucchini or cactus ears

Add the oil to the non-stick skillet and place over a medium flame. When hot, add the beef, onion, and garlic and cook until the beef loses its pink color. Add all other ingredients except for the optional ones and bring to a boil. Reduce the flame to low and simmer, covered, for about 30 minutes. Add the optional ingredients and simmer for about ten more minutes or until the meat is tender. Serves two.

Nutritional information per serving (without optional ingredients): *455 calories (21.8% from fat), 11 g. fat, 56.5 g. protein, 33.4 g. carbohydrates, 129 mgs. cholesterol.*

Dons' Lite Teriyaki

8 ounce sirloin steak, trimmed of all visible fat and cut in one-inch cubes
4 tablespoons bottled Teriyaki sauce
⅓ medium onion, chopped
¼ teaspoon ground ginger
1 cup precooked white rice
2 ounces, juice-packed pineapple chunks

Add the steak, Teriyaki sauce, onion and ginger to a bowl. Mix until steak is evenly coated with sauce. Marinate for 15 minutes.

Place non-stick skillet over medium flame. Add steak with marinade to skillet and cook until done, seven to ten minutes. Add a little water if necessary. Push meat and onions to one side of skillet. Add rice and heat through. About one minute before serving, add pineapple chunks.

Nutritional information per serving: 633 calories (14.2% from fat), 10 g. fat, 53 g. protein, 77.6 g. carbohydrates, 121 mgs. cholesterol.

Let's scoot around the Pacific rim into Thailand.

Thai-Hi Beef

8 ounces sirloin steak, trimmed of all visible fat and cut into small cubes
1 tablespoon sodium-reduced soy sauce
1 heaping teaspoon granulated sugar
¼ teaspoon garlic powder
¼ teaspoon cayenne pepper
½ cup mushrooms, cleaned and sliced
½ teaspoon ground ginger
1 teaspoon peanut oil

   1 small onion, chopped
   1 small sweet red pepper, cut in strips
   1 reduced-sodium beef bouillon cube dissolved in three-quarters
      cup boiling water
   1 teaspoon cornstarch whisked into one tablespoon water
   1 cup precooked rice

In a bowl, combine the sirloin cubes with the soy sauce, sugar, garlic, ginger and cayenne. Set aside. Add the oil to the non-stick skillet and place over a medium-high flame. When hot, add the onion, mushrooms and peppers and sauté until soft, about four to five minutes. With a slotted spoon remove the beef from the sauce and add to the skillet, cooking until browned and stirring often. Add the sauce and when it boils, add the cornstarch mixture. When the sauce returns to the boil, add the rice and cook until heated through.

Suggestion: Pineapple slices make a refreshing and palate-cooling dessert.

Nutritional information per serving: 683 calories (20% from fat), 15.3 g. fat, 57 g. protein, 74.8 g. carbohydrates, 121 mgs. cholesterol.

Lite Curry & Raisins

   ½ cup boiling water
   ½ cup raisins
   1 teaspoon olive oil
   8 ounces sirloin, trimmed of all visible fat and cubed
   1 green onion, chopped
   1 small green bell pepper, chopped
   ½ tablespoon curry powder
   ½ teaspoon salt
   1 tablespoon chopped unsalted peanuts
   1 reduced-sodium beef bouillon cube
   1 cup cooked white rice

In a small dish or bowl, pour the boiling water over the raisins. Set aside.

Add the oil to the skillet and place over a medium flame. When hot, add the beef, onion and green pepper and sauté until meat is browned. Add the curry powder, salt and peanuts and simmer for five minutes.

Drain the raisins (reserve the liquid); add the raisins to the skillet. To reserved raisin juice, add enough water to measure 1/2 cup. Add this and the bouillon cube to skillet and simmer for 15 minutes. Serve over the rice. Serves two.

Nutritional information per serving: 430 calories (22% from fat), 10.5 g. fat, 30.5 g. protein, 55.4 g. carbohydrates, 61 mgs. cholesterol.

Beef LiteSauté

1 teaspoon peanut oil
8 ounces beef tenderloin, trimmed of all visible fat, sliced thin
¼ cup chopped green bell pepper
¼ cup chopped sweet red pepper
¼ cup mushrooms, sliced
½ teaspoon salt
dash of ground black pepper
¼ cup dry red wine
1 cup precooked white rice

Add the oil to a non-stick skillet and place over medium-high flame. Add the tenderloin and brown quickly. Add the peppers and mushrooms and sauté until the mushrooms are soft. Add salt, pepper and wine to skillet. Lower the flame and toss quickly to coat. Serve with the rice on the side.

Nutritional information per serving (including the rice): 713 calories (27.8% from fat), 22.1 g. fat, 50 g. protein, 54.4 g. carbohydrates, 112 mgs. cholesterol.

Yes Soy, Senator, That's A Sirloin

2 tablespoons corn starch
½ cup water
½ cup sodium-reduced soy sauce
2 teaspoons peanut oil
8 ounce sirloin steak, trimmed of all visible fat and sliced thin
3 green onions, sliced into one-inch pieces
1 (6-ounce) can sliced water chestnuts
1 medium green bell pepper, seeded and sliced
2 ounces dried pineapple chunks
1 cup precooked white rice

Add the cornstarch, water and soy sauce to a bowl and stir together until the cornstarch dissolves. Set aside.

Add the oil to the non-stick skillet and place over a medium flame. Add the beef and sauté for about 30 seconds on each side. Add the remaining ingredients and cook four to five minutes. Add the cornstarch mixture to the skillet and stir until thickened. Serve over the rice. Serves two.

Nutritional information per serving: 412 calories (23% from fat), 10.6 g. fat, 31 g. protein, 51.1 g. carbohydrates, 67 mgs. cholesterol.

The cooks in the Ol' West fried just about everything. If they had it, they tossed a steak in the skillet. It was usually one right tough piece of meat. Today, beef is leaner than ever before. If it's aged, lean beef can be quite tender, as long as it isn't cooked well done. Medium is as far as today's leaner beef can be cooked before drying out.

Still, once in a while we like to tickle our tonsils with the flavor of the Ol' West. Here's a leaner version of Western road food.

Yellow Rose LiteSkillet Steak

2 teaspoons olive oil
8 ounce sirloin steak, trimmed of all visible fat
½ cup water
2 tablespoons all-purpose flour
salt and pepper to taste
2 thick slices French bread

Add the olive oil to the non-stick skillet and place over a medium flame. Add the steak. For a medium steak, cook for six minutes, then turn and cook for six minutes more. Once the steak is cooked, remove from the skillet. Add the water to the skillet and slowly stir in the flour to make a gravy. Scrape the skillet bottom to incorporate all of the meat drippings. Season with salt and pepper. Pour the gravy over the steak.

Suggestion: Serve with raw carrots and hard rolls.

Nutritional information per serving (including the bread): 576 calories (24.8% from fat), 15.9 g. fat, 56 g. protein, 48.8 g. carbohydrates, 121 mgs. cholesterol.

LiteStyle Beef Stroganoff

8 ounces beef round steak, trimmed of fat and cut in one-inch cubes
3 tablespoons all-purpose flour
¼ teaspoon black pepper
½ teaspoon sweet paprika
2 teaspoons canola oil
½ cup onion, chopped
1 large garlic clove, minced
4 mushrooms, cleaned and sliced
¼ cup dry red wine or dry sherry
1 packet dry soup mix (mushroom or mixed veggie), reconstituted
½ cup nonfat sour cream
1½ cups medium flat precooked noodles

Place the steak, flour, pepper and paprika in plastic bag and shake to coat. Add the oil to the non-stick skillet and place over medium flame. When hot, add the coated steak and onions and sauté until beef cubes are uniformly brown. Add remaining ingredients except soup and sour cream. Stir and let simmer for about five minutes. Add soup and simmer for another ten minutes. Stir in sour cream and remove from the flame. Dish out steaming hot over the pre-cooked noodles. Serves two.

Nutritional information per serving: 565 calories (19% from fat), 11.9 g. fat, 38 g. protein, 63.4 g. carbohydrates, 112 mgs. cholesterol.

Here's a European version of goulash.

Loaded Goulash

1 teaspoon olive oil
6 ounces sirloin or top round steak, trimmed of all visible fat, cut into half-inch cubes
2 medium onions, chopped
2 celery ribs, sliced thin
1 package dry tomato soup mix (single-serving size)
¾ cup water
salt, black pepper and sweet paprika to taste
8 ounces canned red kidney beans, drained
all-purpose flour

Add the oil to the non-stick skillet and place over a medium-high flame. When hot, add the steak and sauté until it has lost its pink color. Add the onions, celery, soup mix and water. Reduce the flame and simmer gently for 30 minutes. Add the beans and seasonings. Thicken the sauce with flour mixed with a small amount of water, as needed.

Suggestion: Serve this with warm sourdough bread and you'll have a meal you can truly wrap yourself around.

Nutritional information per serving: 713 calories (18.7% from fat), 14.8 g. fat, 54 g. protein, 89.5 g. carbohydrates, 102 mgs. cholesterol.

Pork also can offer some great lite-meal choices. It's important to buy the right type of pork. Pork tenderloin is lean in its own right and any visible fat on the outside is easily stripped away.

One Pan B-B-Q Lite

    6 ounces pork tenderloin, sliced against the grain into quarter-inch medallions
    2 teaspoons canola oil
    1 medium onion, thin sliced
    4 tablespoons barbecue sauce (your choice)
    4 ounces freeze-dried corn prepared according to directions

Heat the non-stick skillet over a medium flame and add the oil. Add the meat and brown until well-cooked. Add the onion and sauté for three or four minutes. Add the barbecue sauce and corn. Cook for another five minutes. Serve.

Note: Prepare the freeze-dried corn in your skillet by adding water and the corn as you are cooking the meat and sauce. Just simmer until the corn is tender.

Nutritional information per serving: 456 calories (24% from fat), 12.2 g. fat, 40 g. protein, 46.4 g. carbohydrates, 111 mgs. cholesterol.

Pork, Pesto, Peppers & Pasta

    6 ounces pork tenderloin, sliced against the grain into quarter-inch medallions
    1 teaspoon canola oil
    1 teaspoon prepared pesto sauce
    1 medium green pepper, julienne sliced
    1 medium red pepper, julienne sliced
    salt and pepper to taste
    1 cup precooked pasta

Heat the non-stick skillet over a medium flame and add the oil and pesto. Stir to spread evenly around the skillet bottom. Add the meat and brown until thoroughly cooked. Stir in the vegetables and sauté until tender. Finally, add the pasta and gently toss for about one minute to reheat.

Note: You may want to add a little extra dried basil to the recipe for a stronger flavor.

Nutritional information per serving: 620 calories (23.8% from fat), 16.4 g. fat, 47 g. protein, 69 g. carbohydrates, 111 mgs. cholesterol.

Dessert

Pancakes, in one form or another, are a favorite dessert around the world. Dessert pancakes are usually thin, sweet and covered with marvelous fruit preserves or powdered sugar. There are many special prepackaged batters available, but you have to watch the nutritional labels. Any pancake batter mix can serve the purpose. Add more water or milk than suggested, because a thinner batter makes delicate, slim pancakes. Roughing it, however, calls for a natural touch. Why not build your own batter? Not only is it a lot of fun, but you'll know all the ingredients.

DJ is half Swede. Here's his family favorite from the Old Country. In Montparnasse, they are called crepes. But to Stockholm Don, it's Plättar.

Plättar Lite

¼ cup nonfat egg substitute
⅔ cup skim milk (reconstituted from powder)
¼ cup instant all-purpose flour
1 tablespoon granulated sugar
1 teaspoon canola oil
pinch of salt (optional)
canola oil

In a bowl, whisk the nonfat egg substitute with the milk, flour, sugar, oil and optional salt. Whisk until the batter is very smooth and lump-free.

Place the non-stick skillet over a medium flame and add a drop or two of oil. When hot, add ⅓ cup of the batter and swirl skillet slightly to spread out as thin as possible. Cook for one to two minutes. With a plastic spatula, lift and turn pancake and cook for one more minute, or until very lightly browned. Remove and continue until no batter remains. Makes three to four Plättars.

Note: If the batter is too thick, add a little more milk. These pancakes should be very thin.

Suggestion: Serve with powdered sugar or strawberry preserves.

Nutritional information per serving: 285 calories (16% from fat), 5.1 g. fat, 14 g. protein, 44.5 g. carbohydrates, 3 mgs. cholesterol.

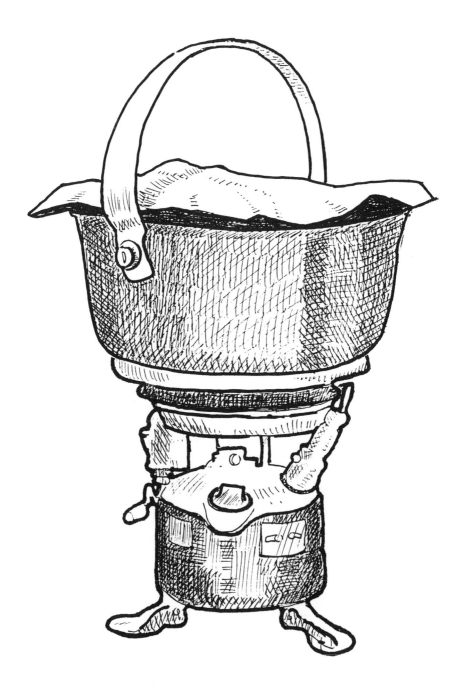

THE POT

The non-stick skillet might be called the trekker's fast-food companion. The pot is a lazier way to turn raw trail food into something palatable. There's no question that the pot is the tool of choice for eating low-fat on the trail.

Before you jump to the conclusion that the standard pot fare starts and ends with soup, remember Grandma's pressure cooker and Mom's crock pot. Both were kettles with an attitude. They could take care of whatever the butcher had on sale and still make your mouth water.

After all, what was on sale in the store usually ended up in the pot in the kitchen. In the "old days" (as today), beef was graded by the fat content. The more marbled the meat, the tenderer the cut (fat is easier to chew than muscle), the higher the cost, and the more infrequent the appearance on the table of the average family. Americans generally followed the European lead, at least until after World War II, of eating more poultry and fish (nightmares of swordfish steak poached in milk), as well as cheaper cuts of red meat. We were eating right because we couldn't afford to do otherwise. We still can't afford to do otherwise. But, today, it's not a question of money.

Lean cuts of meat, by and large, are tough. They demand low heat and plenty of pot time to tenderize. Slow cookin' also lets the flavors of other foods blend and mellow, bringing out all the savory goodness that defines satisfying outdoor cooking.

Most folks who hit the road on bike, canoe or foot can't lug a huge pot around. Usually, a one-quart kettle from a cook kit is about the limit.

There's a lot that can be prepared in a one-quart pot. And, soup is only one, albeit a tasty one, of the possibilities for this versatile vessel. So, before we say "Soup's on," we'll take you on the long tour of the kettle's potential.

The One Pot Breakfast

Breakfast gets you up and stoked for whatever the day holds in store. Cold cereal is certainly the easiest answer for breakfast, but doesn't do much to cut the chill waiting just outside the tent before the morning sun breaks over the horizon. That's the perfect time to pull the one-quart pot out of your mess kit and start building a breakfast that will warm you up just like the sun will later in the day.

Cereals

Here's the question. What's the right food group to give you the calories you need to sustain your energy throughout the morning, without a lot of fat coming along for the ride?

Grains have always been the correct answer.

A morning meal built on grains will keep you going strong throughout a hike or portage. You'll have energy to spare since grains are loaded with complex carbohydrates. Dig in to the following great cereals.

There's something about a steaming bowl of oatmeal that smacks of warm country kitchens, even if you didn't grow up in one. This recipe used to feature ¼ cup of walnuts, which added crunch, flavor and 18 fat grams to the bowl. How to replace walnuts? Since it is crunchy, carries a nut-like flavor and is fat-free, Grape Nuts® cereal is the answer. You get needed calories, without any fat.

Oatmeal with Raisins and Brown Sugar

1½ cups water
⅛ teaspoon salt
⅔ cup old-fashioned oatmeal (not quick)
½ cup seedless raisins
2 tablespoons brown sugar (light or dark, your choice)
¼ cup Grape Nuts® cereal

To a one-quart pot, add water and salt and place the pot over a medium flame. When the water comes to a boil add the oats, stirring slowly to prevent lumping. Reduce the flame to low and cook for five minutes. Add the raisins and cook two minutes, stirring occasionally. When ready to eat, stir in the brown sugar and the Grape Nuts®.

Suggestions: If you enjoy dried fruit, consider substituting golden raisins for regular seedless raisins. Chopped dried apricots are also wonderful in a hot bowl of oatmeal. How about oatmeal with chunks of fresh apple, or with dates, or with applesauce and strawberries, or lightly dusted with ground cinnamon, or drizzled with real pure maple syrup?

Nutritional information per serving: 584 calories (6.9% from fat), 4.5 g. fat, 14 g. protein, 135.4 g. carbohydrates, no cholesterol.

Mandarin Cream of Wheat

2 cups water
¼ teaspoon salt
⅓ cup original Cream of Wheat cereal (not quick)
1 teaspoon ground cinnamon
1 (6-ounce) can water-packed mandarin orange segments, drained

Add the water and salt to a one quart pot and place the pot over a medium flame. When the water begins to boil add the cereal, stirring to prevent lumping. Reduce the flame to low and cook for seven to ten minutes, making sure not to burn the cereal. Add and stir in the cinnamon and oranges.

Nutritional information per serving: *284 calories (2.8% from fat), 0.9 g. fat, 7 g. protein, 62.6 g. carbohydrates, no cholesterol.*

There are many "instant" and "quick" hot cereals available in supermarkets. In our opinion, these fast-cooking cereals sacrifice some of the aesthetic appeal of the longer-cooking varieties. Maybe it's that more finely cut oats tend to result in a gruel-like consistency when prepared. Just as instant soup never has the rich, round, complex flavor of a slowly simmered broth, neither do these "quick" cereals have the same texture as the "real" thing. The extra five minutes needed to cook a non-instant hot cereal makes for a more satisfying meal. Don't forget, there are also some cold cereals like Grape Nuts® and Shredded Wheat that can be prepared as a hot cereal. Their boxes explain exactly how to cook them.

Eggs Etc.

Changing the way we eat often means changing the way we cook. As with the skillet, you can make some superb, low-fat dishes for breakfast in the pot.

You can, of course, always use your pot just like a pan. More than one batch of scrambled eggs has been cooked up in the patrol pot because dinner was still charred onto the skillet. But, the pot opens up all sorts of new eating ideas.

Before you try any of these recipes, take a few moments to think about steam. Steam is terribly hot and can burn you quickly. Treat steam and boiling water just like gasoline and flame.

When you get ready to cook, make sure everything is cold, from the pot and water to the steamer basket and the food. Never place the steamer into boiling water. And, once your meal is cooked, lift the cover off the pot with tongs or an insulated glove to avoid a burn. Never place your face over the pot. After cooking, when things have settled down, remove the steamer and food from the pot using tongs.

Now, on to the etc.

We're lucky today when it comes to sausage. The sausage we ate as kids usually was very high in fat. In fact, a normal breakfast sausage link had on average 12 fat grams. I don't know about you, but my serving size was rarely a single link. Three links was normal, and that piled 36 fat grams on, just for breakfast. Ouch.

Now there are lower fat links available and they are a definite improvement over the past. For example, Jones Dairy Farm makes a "brown and serve" light sausage with only 4.1 fat grams per link. It has a decent flavor and a serving of three links equals the fat of a single link of the high fat version. Hooray for progress.

Leaner Links

3 low-fat sausage links (uncooked or brown and serve)
½ cup water

Place unfrozen links, not touching, in a steamer basket. Add the water to the pot. Place the steamer in the pot and cover. Over a medium flame, bring the water to a boil. Once the water boils, cook "uncooked" links for ten minutes; cook "brown and serve" links for five minutes.

Nutritional information per low-fat link: 55 calories (68.7% from fat), 4.2 g. fat, 3.3 g. protein, 0.5 g. carbohydrates, 24 mgs. cholesterol.

Using some kitchen magic, pork processors have managed to reduce the amount of fat in ham. Some hams can be 99%-lean, with only one percent of the ham's weight coming from fat. It doesn't give us a license to "pig out," but certainly allows us to enjoy the occasional inclusion of ham in our trail meals.

Thinner Ham Sticks

4 ounces cooked, 96%-lean or leaner ham (baked, boiled or
smoked) cut into four-inch sticks
½ cup water

Place the ham sticks, not touching, on a steamer basket. Add the water to the pot. Place the steamer in the pot and cover. Over a medium flame, bring the water to a boil. Once the water boils, cook the ham sticks for five minutes.

Nutritional information per serving: 138 calories (31% from fat), 4.8 g. fat, 22 g. protein, no carbohydrates, 52 mgs. cholesterol.

A high-protein breakfast keeps a healthy body well-fueled for a long time. This is a tasty way to begin a day on the trail and feel energized for hours.

Lean Daybreak Steak

3 tablespoons sodium-reduced soy sauce
1 tablespoon clover honey
¼ pound sirloin or other lean steak, trimmed of all visible fat and sliced thin across the grain
½ cup water

In a small bowl or cup, stir together the soy sauce and honey. Add the sliced steak, stir to coat and marinate for 15 minutes. Place the marinated steak strips on the steamer basket. Add the water to the pot. Place the steamer in the pot and cover. Bring the water to a boil. Cook three minutes for rare to six or seven minutes for well-done.

Nutritional information per serving: 244 calories (17.7% from fat), 4.8 g. fat, 31 g. protein, 22 g. carbohydrates, 60 mgs. cholesterol.

The two Dons use nonfat egg substitutes whenever possible. However, this and a few other recipes could not be preserved without using real, in-the-shell whole eggs. If you follow a low-fat diet regimen (20% or less of daily calories), an egg or two on a single trail breakfast is O.K.

Pablo's Lite Burrito

¼ pound 95%-lean ground beef
1 tablespoon each diced green pepper and onion
pinch salt
pinch ground black pepper
pinch ground sage
vegetable oil spray
2 nonfat flour tortillas
½ cup water
2 large eggs

In a small bowl, mix together the ground beef, onion, green pepper, salt, pepper, and sage. Set aside.

Lightly spray one side of each tortilla with the vegetable oil. Roll each tortilla loosely and place on the steamer. Add the water to the pot, place the steamer in the pot and cover. Place the pot over a medium flame and bring the water to a boil. Once the water boils, remove the pot from the heat and uncover.

Carefully (remember, steam can cause burns) remove the steamer. Unroll the tortillas and lay sprayed side down on a plate. Divide the spiced hamburger mixture between each tortilla. Fold each tortilla over the meat so that it resembles a small pillow. Place the eggs on the steamer. Add additional water to the pot to return the water level to a half a cup. Place the tortillas back on the steamer, folded side down and place steamer inside. Cover and bring to a boil over a medium flame. Once the water boils, lower the flame and cook for 15 minutes.

Nutritional information per serving: 556 calories (25.4% from fat), 15.7 g. fat, 46 g. protein, 55.3 g. carbohydrates, 488 mgs. cholesterol.

The center of any great wilderness breakfast is the chicken egg. The amount of fat in a single large egg is five grams. Even a two-egg breakfast, especially one eaten before an energetic day, can fit within a total controlled fat outdoor diet.

E-Z Hard-Boiled Eggs

   1 to 1½ cups water
   ¼ teaspoon salt
   2 large eggs (cholesterol-reduced, preferred)

Place the water in the pot. Add the salt and eggs. Bring the water to a boil over a medium flame. Reduce the heat so water is just barely bubbling. (Cooking eggs too fast will make them crack and ooze.) Cook for about seven minutes. At higher altitudes, (up to about 10,000 feet), cook ten to 12 minutes. Carefully remove the eggs with a spoon and set aside to cool. (If you have cold water available, the hard-boiled eggs may be placed in a bowl with cold water to accelerate cooling.) Peel and eat.

Nutritional information per serving (two eggs of standard size): 150 calories (60% from fat), 10 g. fat, 12 g. protein, 1.2 g. carbohydrates, 426 mgs. cholesterol.

Incredible edible eggs are the ultimate convenience food. You can just peel and eat them, or slice and dice them with salt and pepper. Try them with some grated reduced-fat or nonfat cheese. Special additives like green onions, pine nuts, basil or a light dusting of real Parmesan cheese can make the good ol' egg a real meal. Get creative.

Nana's Eggs a la Golden Rod

3 hard-boiled eggs
½ cup skim milk
¼ cup all-purpose flour
¼ teaspoon salt (or to taste)
½ to one cup water
salt and ground white pepper, to taste
1 or 2 slices of low-fat, whole grain bread

Peel the eggs and slice each in half. Set one yolk aside and discard the remaining yolks. Slice the egg whites. Set aside. Over a low flame, heat the milk in the pot, taking care not to let it boil. Add the flour and salt to a bowl or cup. Add the water a bit at a time to the flour, while stirring, to make a paste. Slowly add the paste to the heating milk. When the mixture begins to thicken, add the sliced egg whites and white pepper, heating until just hot. Spoon the mixture over the bread. Mash the yolk and sprinkle over the top. Season and serve.

Nutritional information per serving: 265 calories (18.6% from fat), 5.5 g. fat, 21 g. protein, 30.7 g. carbohydrates, 215 mgs. cholesterol.

Poaching eggs on the trail is slightly more difficult than at home. That's because we do them like they are done in restaurants, rather than in little pre-formed pans that turns out rubber eggs. Our way takes a bit more wrist action.

Trailside Poachers

2 cups water
¼ cup white vinegar
2 large eggs (cholesterol-reduced, preferred)

Add the water to the pot and place over a medium to high flame, bringing the water to a boil. Add the vinegar to the water. With a spoon, stir the liquid to create a whirlpool in the center. Add the eggs to the whirlpool. Placing a handle on the pan, continue to swirl the water in a whirlpool. This keeps the eggs from spreading out. Every 15 to 20 seconds, reverse the direction of the whirlpool by rocking the pot in the opposite direction. After three to four minutes, remove the eggs from the pan.

Suggestions: Serve the poached eggs over low-fat whole-grain bread, split, whole-grain rolls, or hot low-fat hash, etc.

Nutritional information per serving (with standard eggs): 150 calories (60% from fat), 10 g. fat, 12 g. protein, 1.2 g. carbohydrates, 426 mgs. cholesterol.

Poached eggs are the number one ingredient in a special egg dish...Eggs Benedict. This dish usually requires Hollandaise sauce. It is possible to make Hollandaise sauce on the trail, but you need a double boiler. That's usually too much to carry. Substitute this low-fat cheese sauce, instead.

Cheese Sauce Lite

2 tablespoons all-purpose flour
¼ cup water
¼ cup skim milk
1 tablespoon diet margarine
1 ounce shredded, nonfat sharp or cheddar cheese
salt and pepper to taste

In a cup or small bowl, stir together the flour and water to form a paste, set aside. Add the milk to the pot and place over a medium flame. Add margarine to melt, stirring frequently. Add the flour mixture gradually, while stirring, to thicken the sauce. Add the cheese, salt and pepper. Continue to heat until the cheese has melted. Set aside and cover.

Nutritional information per recipe: 136 calories (14.5% from fat), 2.2 g. fat, 10 g. protein, 17.2 g. carbohydrates, 1 mg. cholesterol.

Benedict's Eggs

1 English muffin, split, toasted, cooled and placed in a resealable sandwich bag
2 fresh poached eggs (see recipe above)
2 slices Canadian bacon
1 recipe Cheese Sauce Lite (see above)

Remove the English muffins from the plastic bag and place each half, cut side up, on a plate. Lay a slice of Canadian bacon on each half. Place a poached egg on each half. Spoon the hot cheese sauce over all.

Nutritional information per serving: 515 calories (30% from fat), 17.2 g. fat, 29 g. protein, 29.2 g. carbohydrates, 454 mgs. cholesterol.

Dining Out In A Pot

Dining out of doors should be an experience of great food combined with remarkable atmosphere...not unlike a meal in a four-star restaurant. Using your pot to cook low-fat meals, however, means changing how you approach filling up.

First, lose your watch. Unless you have to rendezvous with part of your crew at a specific time and place, there's no particular reason why you should have to hurry your meal. If there is, you probably shouldn't be cooking.

Second, and more important, turning to the pot means getting creative. Trail-side food should hit the senses with aromas and flavors that enhance the whole trekking adventure. Use your spice rack and your brain. Be patient and enjoy the outcome.

Chicken

Chicken is wonderful, and the best part of the chicken is the breast. Why? It is lowest in fat. Does this make a big difference? Huge. Dark meat has more than twice as much fat as light. For healthier, lower-fat eating on the road, chicken breast served up in a tasty manner is worth whatever effort went into its preparation.

Remember, the majority of the fat in a chicken is found in the skin. One ounce of light chicken meat has 0.5 fat grams. That same ounce including the skin has 3.1 fat grams. So, stripping the skin from an average four-ounce chicken breast strips it of more than ten fat grams, but leaves plenty of flavor behind. Slow cooking a chicken breast in any liquid means that the moisture in the breast meat will remain. That's why your pot and chicken breast make such beautiful music together.

Chicken with Stuffing

   1 teaspoon olive oil
   1 medium onion, diced
   ½ cup green pepper, chopped
   1 small tomato, diced
   1 stalk celery, chopped
   8-ounce skinless, boneless chicken breast, cubed
   salt and pepper to taste
   1 reduced-sodium chicken bouillon cube
   ½ cup water
   ½ cup herb-seasoned bread cubes

Place the pot over a medium flame. Add the olive oil, and when hot, add and sauté the onions, green pepper, tomato and celery until tender. Add the chicken and cook five minutes, or until almost cooked through. Add the salt and pepper, bouillon cube and water. Continue cooking and stirring until the bouillon cube dissolves. Add the bread cubes and stir until they absorb the liquid and are soft.

Suggestion: Rice may be substituted for the bread cubes—just cover the pot and let it sit, off the flame, for a few minutes. Also, cooking time will vary depending on the stove and altitude.

Nutritional information per serving: 580 calories (16.3% from fat), 10.5 g. fat, 63 g. protein, 55.7 g. carbohydrates, 137 mgs. cholesterol.

This is almost a chicken stew, but with a wonderful flavor and character all its own.

Chicken in the Pot

1 carrot, cut into small chunks
½ rib celery, strings removed and sliced
½ medium onion, sliced
1 medium potato, diced
1 chicken-flavored bouillon cube
½ cup water
1 whole chicken breast, split, skinned and boned
¼ teaspoon dried thyme leaves, crumbled
¼ teaspoon salt
⅛ teaspoon pepper

Place all the vegetables, bouillon cube and water in the pot. Place the pot over a medium flame and bring to a boil, stirring often. Reduce the flame to low and stir in the chicken, salt, pepper and thyme. Cover and continue to cook, at a simmer, for 30 minutes or until the chicken is done. Add water, as needed, to keep the broth level up.

Nutritional information per serving: 477 calories (6.9% from fat), 3.7 g. fat, 60 g. protein, 49 g. carbohydrates, 137 mgs. cholesterol.

Pepper Pot Chicken

1½ teaspoons canola oil
1 small onion, diced
½ tablespoon sweet paprika
½ pound chicken breast, skinned and boned
½ teaspoon salt

¼ **teaspoon black pepper**
1 **medium sweet green pepper, cored, seeded and diced**
1 **medium sweet red pepper, cored, seeded and diced**
¾ **cup water**
4 **ounces nonfat cream cheese, cut into cubes**

Add the oil to the pot and place over a medium flame. When the oil is hot, but not smoking, add the onions and cook, stirring, for five to six minutes or until lightly browned. Stir in the paprika and chicken, add the water. Cover the pot, reduce the flame to low and slowly simmer for 20 minutes. Stir in the salt, pepper and sweet peppers. Cover and simmer for 15 minutes, stirring occasionally. Add the cream cheese, a cube at a time, while stirring, until it melts and mixes into the sauce.

Suggestions: Serve with chunks of sourdough or whole grain bread. This also goes great over pasta or rice.

Nutritional information per serving: 512 calories (17.6% from fat), 10 g. fat, 75 g. protein, 23.4 g. carbohydrates, 142 mgs. cholesterol.

Sometimes a side dish makes a whole meal, as in the following.

Pepp R'D Cheese-Mac

3 **cups water**
1 **teaspoon salt**
4 **ounces dry macaroni elbows (about two hands full)**
¼ **cup skim milk**
½ **cup fat-reduced mild cheddar cheese**
¼ **teaspoon hot red pepper flakes**
¼ **teaspoon salt**
⅛ **teaspoon black pepper**
½ **teaspoon black walnut flavoring**

Add the water and one teaspoon of salt to the pot and place over a high flame. When the water begins boiling, add the macaroni, stirring to make certain the elbows don't stick together.

Reduce the flame to medium and cook for seven to eight minutes. Drain the macaroni and discard the water.

Reduce the flame to low, add the milk and cheese to the pot and return to the flame. While stirring, add the cooked macaroni and the remaining seasonings. Stir until the cheese melts.

Nutritional information per serving: 603 calories (17.7% from fat), 11.9 g. fat, 34 g. protein, 88.2 g. carbohydrates, 1 mg. cholesterol.

Pasta and chicken just seem to be a natural combination for the low-fat trekker. Pasta packs the carbos your body needs for quick-burn calories. Chicken is a protein source and is low in slow-burning fat, to boot.

Primary Poulet and Pasta

1½ teaspoons olive oil
1 lemon, juiced
¼ teaspoon each dried basil, dried oregano, ground black pepper and garlic powder
salt to taste
½ boneless, skinless chicken breast (about 4 oz.), cut into chunks
1 medium sweet green pepper, core and seeds removed, diced
1 medium sweet red pepper, core and seeds removed, diced
1 carrot, peeled and diced
½ cup green peas
1 cup precooked macaroni
1 tablespoon grated Parmesan cheese

In a bowl, stir together the oil, lemon juice, spices and salt. Add the chicken and stir to coat. Cover and let sit for ten minutes.

Over a medium flame, heat the pot and place the drained chicken in to brown and cook. Reserve the marinade. Tend regularly to avoid burning. When the chicken is white throughout (10 to 12 minutes), add the marinade and the vegetables to the pot and sauté for two to three minutes only. Add the macaroni and warm for one minute more. Remove from the flame and add the cheese. Toss to mix. Serve.

Nutritional information per serving: 492 calories (20% from fat), 11 g. fat, 38 g. protein, 61.2 g. carbohydrates, 72 mgs. cholesterol.

Sweet and Spicy Chicken

1 large carrot, peeled and sliced
1 large potato, peeled and sliced
1 medium green pepper, cored, seeded and sliced into spears
3 tablespoons water
1 tablespoon light brown sugar
½ teaspoon salt
½ teaspoon hot curry powder (or to taste)
¼ teaspoon black pepper
1 whole chicken breast, split, skinned, boned and cut in half

Place the vegetables and water in the pot and stir. In a cup, mix together the sugar, salt, curry powder and pepper. Coat the chicken with the seasoning mixture. Place the chicken on top of the vegetables and cover the pot. Place the pot over a medium flame and when the water boils, lower the flame and simmer for about 40 minutes. Additional water may need to be added from time to time to avoid scorching.

Nutritional information per serving: 573 calories (5.7% from fat), 3.6 g. fat, 62 g. protein, 73.8 g. carbohydrates, 136 mgs. cholesterol.

East Indian Express Lite Chicken

2 teaspoons canola oil
1 medium onion, chopped fine
1 rib celery, chopped fine
½ pound skinless, boneless chicken breast, cubed
⅓ cup all-purpose flour (not self-rising)
2 reduced-sodium chicken bouillon cubes, dissolved in 1 1/2 cups water
1 (6-ounce) can tomato juice
½ teaspoon Worcestershire sauce
1 teaspoon hot curry powder (or to taste)

Add the oil to the pot and place over a medium flame. When hot, add the onion and celery and cook, stirring, until soft, about five minutes. Add the chicken and cook until it loses its pink color, stirring occasionally. Add the flour and stir to coat. Add the bouillon cubes and water and cook until the bouillon dissolves and the sauce is smooth and thick. Add the tomato juice, curry powder and Worcestershire sauce. Cover and simmer for five minutes.

Suggestion: Serve over pre-cooked rice.

Nutritional information per serving: 627 calories (19.2% from fat), 13.4 g. fat, 61 g. protein, 60 g. carbohydrates, 138 mgs. cholesterol.

Chicken España

½ pound skinless, boneless chicken breast, cubed
2 teaspoons olive oil
1 vine-ripened tomato, cubed
1 medium sweet green pepper, diced
1 medium onion, chopped
1 (6-ounce) can tomato paste

¾ **cup water**
¼ **teaspoon salt**
¼ **teaspoon cayenne pepper**
black pepper, to taste
¾ **cup instant rice**
¼ **cup ripe olives, diced (optional)**

Add the oil to the pot and place over a medium flame. When the oil is hot, but not smoking, add the chicken and sauté for ten minutes. Add the tomato, green pepper, and onion and sauté six minutes more. Stir in the tomato paste, water, salt, cayenne and black pepper. Bring the sauce to a low simmer while stirring. Add the rice and stir in. Cover, remove from the flame and set aside for five minutes. Serve garnished with the olives. Serves two.

Nutritional information per serving (including optional olives): 502 calories (14.9% from fat), 8.4 g. fat, 33 g. protein, 70.6 g. carbohydrates, 68 mgs. cholesterol.

Big Red Bird

2 **teaspoons olive oil**
1 **whole chicken breast, split, skinned, boned and cut into chunks**
1 **medium onion, diced**
1 **clove garlic, crushed**
3 **large mushrooms, sliced**
1 **very ripe tomato, crushed**
1 **cup water**
1 **(6-ounce) can tomato paste**
½ **teaspoon dried oregano, crumbled**
¼ **teaspoon dried basil, crumbled**
¼ **teaspoon black pepper**
¼ **teaspoon fennel seed**
1 **teaspoon granulated sugar**
1½ **cups pre-cooked spaghetti**
1 **tablespoon grated Parmesan cheese**

Add the oil to the pot and place over a medium flame. Add the chicken. Stir and cook until lightly browned on all sides. Add the onion and garlic and cook until the onion begins to soften, two to three minutes. Add the mushrooms and tomatoes and cook for two minutes more. Add the remaining ingredients except for the spaghetti. Stir until the tomato paste dissolves, reduce the flame to low, cover and simmer for about 30 minutes. Taste and adjust the seasoning. Serve over the spaghetti, or stir the spaghetti into the sauce at the end. Dust with the cheese and serve. Serves two.

Suggestions: This makes a dynamic spaghetti sauce without the chicken. You also can add a bay leaf to seasoning, or sauté some chopped sweet green pepper along with the onion.

Nutritional information per serving: 460.5 calories (17% from fat), 8.7 g. fat, 36 g. protein, 58.7 g. carbohydrates, 70 mgs.

Here's another favorite that keeps the chicken and veggies theme going. It's one of the tastiest bits of straight line cooking you whip up outside. And it's really loaded with carbos!

Litestyle Chicken Moussaka

1 whole chicken breast, split, skinned, boned and cut into cubes
2 teaspoons olive oil
salt and pepper, to taste
1 small eggplant, trimmed and cubed
1 medium green pepper, core and seeds removed, diced
1 medium white onion, trimmed and diced
1 medium summer squash, trimmed and diced
½ teaspoon each dried basil, dried oregano and dried rosemary
1 (6-ounce) can tomato paste
¼ cup dried lentils
1½ cups water
½ teaspoon fennel seeds

Heat the pot over a medium flame and add the oil. Add the chicken cubes and, while stirring, cook until light brown. Add the salt and pepper., then the vegetables. Cook until vegetables are tender, about five minutes. Season with basil, oregano and rosemary. Add the tomato paste, lentils and water and bring to low boil, stirring. Reduce the flame to low and simmer for 15 minutes. Add and stir in the fennel seeds. Simmer for five more minutes, or until the lentils are tender. Add water to smooth the sauce, if necessary. Serve.

Nutritional information per serving: 801 calories (16.5% from fat), 14.7 g. fat, 76 g. protein, 95 g. carbohydrates, 136 mgs. cholesterol.

Clark Street Chicken

3 tablespoon all-purpose flour (not self-rising)
1 tablespoon dry mustard
1 teaspoon black pepper
1 whole chicken breast, split, skinned, boned and cut into strips
2 teaspoons canola oil

   1 medium onion, chopped
   1 cup water
   ½ one-quart-sized packet of powdered skim milk
   1 tablespoon all-purpose flour
   1 ripe tomato, sliced thin
   1 rib celery, chopped
   1 tablespoon fresh parsley, chopped
   1 dill pickle, chopped

Combine the three tablespoons of flour, mustard and pepper in a plastic bag. Add the chicken strips, seal the bag and shake until the chicken is coated. Set aside.

Add the oil to the pot and place over a medium flame. When the oil is hot, but not smoking, add the chicken. Stir and cook until lightly browned, about six minutes. Add the onion and continue cooking until the onion is soft, about five minutes.

While the onion is cooking, stir the milk powder and one tablespoon of flour into the water until dissolved. When the onion is soft, add the milk powder/flour mixture to the pot. Heat to a boil, taking care not to burn. Stir in the tomato and celery. Reduce the flame to very low, cover and simmer gently, stirring occasionally, for 20 to 25 minutes. Garnish with sprinkled parsley and pickle. Serve.

Suggestion: A Kaiser or cloverleaf roll makes a great accompaniment.

Nutritional information per serving: 780 calories (18.8% from fat), 16.3 g. fat, 77 g. protein, 76 g. carbohydrates, 144 mgs. cholesterol.

Agaricaceae Bird

   1½ teaspoons canola oil
   ½ cup sliced fresh mushrooms
   ½ medium onion, chopped fine
   2 reduced-sodium chicken bouillon cubes
   1 cup water
   1 whole chicken breast, split, skinned and boned
   dried oregano, to taste
   black pepper, to taste
   ½ cup uncooked Minute Rice®
   1 carrot, cut into thin curls

Add the oil to the pot and place over a medium flame. Add the mushrooms and onions, and cook, stirring, until tender. Add the water and bouillon cubes. Bring to a boil, stirring. Reduce the flame to low and place the chicken on top of the vegetables. Season with the oregano and pepper. Cover and cook for 35 minutes. Remove the chicken and add the rice, stirring to mix.

Return the chicken to the pot, distribute the carrots over all, cover and cook for five minutes more. Remove pot from flame and allow to rest covered, for five minutes. Serve.

Nutritional information per serving: 763 calories (13.2% from fat), 11.2 g. fat, 63 g. protein, 94.4 g. carbohydrates, 138 mgs. cholesterol.

Mo' Chicken Peas

1½ teaspoons canola oil
1 whole chicken breast, split, skinned and boned and cut into chunks
1 medium onion, chopped
¾ cup water
1 reduced-sodium chicken bouillon cube
¾ cup freeze-dried peas
salt and pepper to taste
1 tablespoon all-purpose flour
¼ cup water

Add the oil to the pot and place over a medium flame. When the oil is hot, but not smoking, add the chicken. Stir and cook until the chicken is light brown, about seven to eight minutes. Add the onion and cook until softened, about five minutes. Add the remaining ingredients except for the flour and quarter-cup of water, stirring until combined. Lower the flame, cover the pot and gently simmer for about 25 minutes. In a cup, stir together the flour and water. Add to the pot and stir to combine, simmer five minutes more. Serve.

Nutritional information per serving: 550 calories (17% from fat), 10.4 g. fat, 64 g. protein, 45 g. carbohydrates, 137 mgs. cholesterol.

The Bird King and Pasta

1½ cups water
2 reduced-sodium chicken bouillon cubes
1 whole chicken breast, split, skinned, boned and cut into chunks
3 ounces nonfat cream cheese, cut into cubes
½ cup freeze-dried peas

2 tablespoons all-purpose flour
1 sweet red pepper, cored, seeded and diced
1 cup pre-cooked noodles or elbow macaroni

Add the water and bouillon cubes to the pot and bring to a boil over a medium flame, stirring occasionally. Add the chicken, cream cheese (a cube at a time), peas, flour and red pepper. Stir until the cream cheese melts. Reduce the flame to low, cover and gently simmer, stirring occasionally, for 25 minutes. Add the noodles, stir to combine, cover, remove from the flame and let sit for five minutes. Serve.

Nutritional information per serving: 742 calories (6.2% from fat), 5.1 g. fat, 88 g. protein, 76.7 g. carbohydrates, 153 mgs. cholesterol.

New-Fashioned Lite Chicken Fricassee

¾ cup water (or enough to cover chicken)
1 whole chicken breast, split, skinned and boned
¾ cup skim milk (or powdered skim milk and water in 1:3 ratio)
1½ teaspoons all-purpose flour
½ teaspoon salt
¼ teaspoon black pepper
1 cup precooked noodles

Add the water and chicken to the pot. Add sufficient water to cover the chicken by a quarter-inch. Place the pot over a medium flame and when the water begins to boil, lower the flame and gently simmer the chicken for 20 minutes. In a cup, stir together the milk and flour. Add the flour mixture to the pot and stir until combined. Add the salt and pepper. Cook and stir until thickened, about two minutes. Serve over the precooked noodles.

Suggestion: Fresh carrot sticks add crunch and color to the meal.

Nutritional information per serving: 550 calories (9.3% from fat), 5.7 g. fat, 68 g. protein, 51.5 g. carbohydrates, 191 mgs. cholesterol.

Heat and food don't necessarily have to go hand-in-hand. Here's a neat recipe that makes a great cold meal on a hot day.

LoFat's Chicken Salad

2 tablespoons clover honey
2 tablespoons nonfat mayonnaise
1 lemon, juiced
¼ teaspoon onion salt
1 rib celery, diced
3 packets of mustard
½ pound cooked white meat chicken, diced
1 (8-ounce) can sliced water chestnuts, drained

In your pot, use a spoon to mix all the ingredients together except the chicken and water chestnuts. Once combined, add the chicken and water chestnuts, stirring and tossing to coat.

Suggestion: Some hard rolls or slices of French bread are excellent with this salad.

Nutritional information per serving: 538 calories (10.2% from fat), 6.1 g. fat, 56 g. protein, 65.8 g. carbohydrates, 136 mgs. cholesterol.

Jill's Rice Salad

Jill Seals, world-class kayaker, feeds a larger version of this salad to groups she guides down California's Kern River. Our thanks to Jill for sharing this great one-pot, low-fat salad.

1 cup precooked brown or white rice
1 green onion, chopped
2 radishes, chopped
½ cup bean spouts, diced
1 stalk celery, diced
1 medium green bell pepper, diced
5 small olives, pitted and chopped
1 small tomato, diced
¼ cup shredded reduced-fat cheddar or other sharp cheese
3 tablespoons balsamic vinegar
½ teaspoon Mrs. Dash seasoning

Add all of the ingredients to the pot except for the vinegar and Mrs. Dash, mixing until combined. In a cup, mix the vinegar and Mrs. Dash seasoning. Pour the dressing over salad and toss until coated. Serve.

Nutritional information per serving: 360 calories (18.8% from fat), 7.5 g. fat, 16 g. protein, 57.5 g. carbohydrates, no cholesterol.

Here's The Beef

As we said earlier, your kettle lets you use less expensive and tougher cuts of meat, thanks to the wonderful tenderizing properties of cooking for 30 minutes or more. We're not saying you want to use meat that's less than the best. Rather, it's a way to cut back on the notorious fat grams found in the majority of red meats. In the pot, it's the cooking that makes the meat chewable, not the fat content.

You can visit almost any market and find USDA-graded Select beef. Prime is the top grade, Choice is second and Select is third. Meat is graded on how much it is marbled by fat. You can trim fat from the outside of Prime, Choice and Select cuts of beef, but you can't remove the fat from the interior. Thus, four ounces of broiled top round yields 10.1 grams of fat (Prime), 6.7 grams (Choice) or 4.2 grams (Select). The "choice" is obvious.

La Vache In The Pot

½ pound boneless beef top round, trimmed of all visible fat and cut into strips across the grain
3 tablespoons all-purpose flour
2 teaspoons canola oil

Select one of the following sauces:

Tomato Sauce

1 green pepper, diced
½ cup water
1 large tomato, crushed
1 teaspoon dried onion flakes
¼ teaspoon sweet paprika
salt and pepper to taste

Mushroom and Potato Sauce

3 large white mushrooms, sliced
1 medium potato, sliced thin
1 cup water
⅔ cup powdered skim milk or one cup skim milk
1 tablespoon all-purpose flour
ground black pepper to taste

Onion and Garlic Sauce
  1 carrot, chopped
  1 tablespoon granulated sugar
  1 cup water
  1 tablespoon all-purpose flour
  1 teaspoon dried onion flakes
  ¼ teaspoon garlic powder
  salt and pepper to taste

To prepare the meat: Add the flour and beef to a plastic bag. Securely close bag and shake beef until coated. In the pot, over a medium flame, heat the oil and brown the coated meat. (Since the beef is coated with flour, it is easier to burn the meat. Keep a careful eye on the pot while the meat is cooking.)

For the tomato sauce: Add the green pepper to the pot with the beef and cook until tender, about four to five minutes.

For the mushroom and potato sauce: Add the mushrooms and potatoes to beef in the pot.

For the onion and garlic sauce: Add and cook the carrot, then add the sugar to caramelize both the vegetable and the beef.

At this point, add all other ingredients for the sauce base you selected. Reduce the flame and cover the pot. Simmer for 35 to 45 minutes, stirring occasionally to prevent sticking. Add water, from time to time, to keep the sauce from getting too thick.

Suggestion: Any of the above is absolutely wonderful served over cooked rice or pasta. Add a couple of hard rolls to mop up any remaining sauce. An uncooked vegetable, served on the side, fills out this low-fat meal very nicely.

Nutritional information per serving for beef with Tomato Sauce: 459 calories (24.9% from fat), 12.7 g. fat, 56 g. protein, 29.1 g. carbohydrates, 128 mgs. cholesterol.

Nutritional information per serving for beef with Mushroom and Potato Sauce: 706 calories (16.8% from fat), 13.2 g. fat, 67 g. protein, 76.5 g. carbohydrates, 132 mgs. cholesterol.

Nutritional information per serving for beef with Onion and Garlic Sauce: 547 calories (27.4% from fat), 16.7 g. fat, 56 g. protein, 41.7 g. carbohydrates, 128 mgs. cholesterol.

The pot is truly a vessel of many tongues. Here's a Franco-Italian favorite.

Savoyard Roast

> 2 tablespoons Dijon-style mustard (any favorite mustard may be
>   substituted)
> ½ teaspoon garlic powder
> ½ teaspoon dried basil leaves, crumbled
> ½ pound beef top round, trimmed of all visible fat
> 2 teaspoons olive oil
> 1 cup water
> 1 medium sweet green pepper, cored, seeded and cut into strips
> 1 medium sweet red pepper, cored, seeded and cut into strips
> 1 large potato, unpeeled, but sliced
> 1 medium onion, chopped

In a cup, stir together the mustard, garlic powder and basil. Rub the outside of the meat with the mixture. Heat the pot over a medium flame and add the oil. Add the meat and brown on all sides. Add the water, lower the flame, cover the pot and simmer for about one hour, stirring occasionally. Add the vegetables, cover and simmer for another 30 minutes. Serve.

Suggestion: Serve with dense Italian rolls (since they make great sponges for the sauce).

*Nutritional information per serving: 676 calories (25% from fat), 18.8 g. fat,
58 g. protein, 64.1 g. carbohydrates, 128 mgs. cholesterol.*

We can't leave the rich Mediterranean area without dipping into a bowl of spaghetti swimming in a sauce that...well... This ingredient list may be long, but read on and savor.

Four Star Spaghetti

> ½ pound 95%-lean ground beef
> 1 teaspoon olive oil
> 1 medium onion, diced
> 1 clove garlic, crushed
> 1 sweet green pepper, core and seeds removed, diced
> 1 large ripe tomato, core removed and the rest crushed
> 1 (6 ounce) can tomato paste
> 1 cup water

1 teaspoon dried oregano leaves, crumbled
½ teaspoon dried basil leaves, crumbled
1 tablespoon granulated sugar
1 tablespoon grated Parmesan cheese
salt and pepper to taste
1½ cups precooked pasta

Add the ground beef to the pot and place over a low flame. Brown and break up the beef. Drain off any fat, add the oil and increase the flame to medium. Add the onion, garlic and green pepper and sauté until the onions are soft. Add the remaining ingredients except for the pasta, stirring to combine. Lower the flame and gently simmer for 25 minutes. Mix in the pasta. Remove from the flame and serve with a green salad with nonfat dressing. Serves two.

Nutritional information per serving: 460 calories (20.6% from fat), 11.5 g. fat, 33.5 g. protein, 59.6 g. carbohydrates, 64 mgs. cholesterol.

Cross over the Alps into France. The following recipe began life using only vegetables. It's the French homemaker's answer to cleaning out the fridge. DJ soon discovered that lean beef made an interesting and tasty difference. If you wish to return this dish to its vegetarian roots, substitute two cups of sliced white mushrooms for the meat. Substitute veggies freely either in the meat or meatless versions.

Biftek Ratatouille

1 teaspoon olive oil
½ pound beef eye of the round, trimmed of all visible fat and sliced thin
1 medium onion, peeled and sliced
1 clove garlic, crushed
1 sweet green pepper, cored, seeded and diced
1 summer or zucchini squash, top trimmed and sliced
1 medium eggplant, top trimmed and diced
1 medium tomato, cored and cut into chunks
1 (6 ounce) can tomato paste
1 cup water
2 tablespoons granulated sugar
1 medium bay leaf
¼ teaspoon fennel seed
salt and pepper to taste

Add the oil to the pot and place over a medium flame. When the oil is hot, but not smoking, add the steak. Cook until it has lost its pink color. Add the onions and sauté until soft. Add the remaining ingredients. Cover, reduce the flame to low and cook for about 35 minutes, stirring often, or until the sauce thickens. For a fancy touch, add a tablespoon of grated Parmesan or Romano cheese.

Nutritional information per serving: 745 calories (20.2% from fat), 16.7 g. fat, 59 g. protein, 96 g. carbohydrates, 121 mgs. cholesterol.

Let's travel out to the French countryside and use a little of what the French are best known for—wine.

Biftek with Wine

¼ cup all-purpose flour
½ pound top sirloin, cut into one-inch chunks
1 teaspoon canola oil
1 medium onion, chopped
1 clove garlic, diced fine
1 packet Lipton Cup-A-Soup® cream of mushroom soup mix
1 cup water
¼ cup dry red wine (not cooking wine, drinkable wine)
salt and pepper to taste
1½ cups pre-cooked noodles

Add the flour and meat to a plastic bag. Seal the bag and shake until the beef is coated with flour.

Add the oil to the pot and place over a medium flame. Add the beef and cook until lightly browned. Add the onion and garlic and sauté until tender. Add the remaining ingredients, except for the noodles, and stir until combined. Bring to a boil. Reduce the flame to low, cover and simmer for 35 minutes. Serve over the noodles. Serves two.

Suggestion: Some dense French bread is a perfect accompaniment. Bon Appetit!

Nutritional information per serving: 469 calories (19.9% from fat), 10.3 g. fat, 30.2 g. protein, 54.5 g. carbohydrates, 69 mgs. cholesterol.

A trip to Mexico makes for a tasty south-of-the-border meal in a pot.

Rio Grande Rice

½ pound 95%-lean ground beef
1 medium onion, chopped
1 small to medium mild green pepper, chopped
3 plum tomatoes, crushed
½ cup water
½ cup uncooked long-grain white rice
½ teaspoon chili powder (more if you like things spicy)
salt and pepper to taste

Add the ground beef to the pot and place over a medium flame. Cook, breaking up the meat with the edge of spoon, until the beef loses its pink color. Pour off any fat. Add the remaining ingredients; stir until well-combined. Bring to simmer, cover, reduce the flame and cook for about 20 minutes or until the rice is tender.

Nutritional information per serving: 759 calories (15.2% from fat), 12.8 g. fat, 56 g. protein, 119.7 g. carbohydrate, 124 mgs. cholesterol.

Back to the good ol' U.S.A. Though no one seems to know for certain, chili seems to have originated in the Southwest. Regardless of location, everyone has a favorite chili recipe. This one is ours.

"No Beans About It" Chili

1 teaspoon canola oil
½ pound beef sirloin, trimmed of all visible fat and cut into bite-sized chunks
1 large onion, chopped
1 clove garlic, crushed
1 medium tomato, chopped
4 large mushrooms, sliced
½ cup dehydrated corn
1 (6 ounce) can of tomato paste
¾ cup water
1½ teaspoons chili powder
½ teaspoon ground cumin
¼ teaspoon black pepper
salt to taste

Add the oil to the pot and place over a medium flame. When the oil is hot, add the beef, stir and cook until lightly browned. Add all the remaining ingredients, cover, reduce the flame and simmer until the corn is tender, about 20 minutes.

Suggestion: Pita (pocket) bread, the great no-fat-added flat bread from the Mediterranean, adds complex carbohydrates to this meal without adding any fat. It also brings the fat calories to below 20 percent.

Nutritional information per serving: 732 calories (24% from fat), 19.7 g. fat, 57 g. protein, 86 g. carbohydrates, 137 mgs. cholesterol.

Remember going through the cafeteria line at school and spying stuffed peppers? We sure do. We also remembered how we loved them. Here are two great ways to prepare peppers on the trail.

Bold & Beefy Peppers

   8 ounces 95%-lean ground beef
   1 large onion, split (dice half, slice other half a quarter-inch thick)
   ⅔ cup instant rice, uncooked
   1 medium tomato, cored and diced
   ¼ cup nonfat egg substitute
   ¼ teaspoon hot pepper sauce
   garlic salt and ground black pepper to taste
   2 medium sweet green peppers, tops cut off and seeds removed
   ½ cup water

In a bowl, mix together the ground beef, diced onion, rice, tomato, egg substitute, garlic salt, hot pepper sauce and black pepper until well combined. Divide the stuffing evenly and pack each pepper. Place the onion slices on the bottom of pot. Place the peppers upright in the pot, on top of the onion slices, and add the water. Cover. Over a medium flame, bring the water to a boil. Reduce the flame to low and cook for 45 minutes. Check to maintain water level; it should be about one inch up the sides of the peppers.

Suggestion: Serve this with slices of fresh tomato.

Nutritional information per serving: 911 calories (12.5% from fat), 12.7 g. fat, 65 g. protein, 131 g. carbohydrates, 124 mgs. cholesterol.

Since meat can spoil easily on the trail, here's a great way to stuff peppers that employs rice as the substance and cheese for flavor. Tasty...very tasty.

"No-Beef-About-It" Stuffed Peppers

1 large onion (dice half, slice the remaining into quarter-inch thick slices)
¾ cup precooked wild rice
½ cup precooked long-grain white rice
1 medium tomato, diced
¼ cup seasoned bread crumbs
¼ cup nonfat egg substitute
3 ounces reduced-fat sharp cheddar cheese
¼ cup green olives, chopped
salt and pepper to taste
2 medium sweet green peppers, tops cut off and seeds removed
½ cup water

In a bowl, mix together all the ingredients except for the peppers, onion slices and water. Divide the mixture evenly and stuff the peppers. Place the onion slices on the bottom of the pot. Place the stuffed peppers on top of the onions and carefully add the water. Cover and place over a medium flame. Bring the water to a boil, reduce the flame to low and simmer for 45 minutes. Check the water level to make certain it remains about a quarter-inch up the sides of the peppers.

Nutritional information per serving: 783 calories (20.6% from fat), 17.9 g. fat, 46 g. protein, 109.2 g. carbohydrates, 15 mgs. cholesterol.

Mrs. MacGuire's Boiled Dinner

½ pound lean corned beef brisket, rinsed, trimmed of all visible fat and tightly wrapped
water
¼ head cabbage
1 large onion, peeled and cut into quarters
2 medium potatoes, cut in half
2 carrots, peeled and cut into chunks
½ teaspoon celery flakes
1 medium bay leaf
ground black pepper to taste

Unwrap the corned beef and place in the bottom of the pot. Add water to the pot until the beef is covered by a half-inch. Place the pot over a medium flame and bring to a boil. Reduce the flame to low, cover and gently simmer for about one hour, making sure that the water does not boil away.

Drain off the water and add the remaining ingredients. Cover the meat and vegetables with fresh water. Return the flame to medium and bring to a gentle boil; reduce the flame to low, cover and cook for about 25 minutes or until the potatoes pierce easily with a fork.

Nutritional information per serving: 860 calories (18.3% from fat), 17.5 g. fat, 61 g. protein, 117.5 g. carbohydrates, 139 mgs. cholesterol.

Many lean cuts of meat have the benefit of being inexpensive and the downside of being tough. Here's where your pot comes to the rescue. Simmer lean but tough meats for a while, and you'll find some very good eating when the pot is finally uncovered.

Just a Cotton-Pickin' Minute Steak

　　1 or 2 cube steaks (8 ounces, total)
　　salt and pepper to taste
　　garlic powder to taste
　　1 medium onion, sliced
　　½ cup instant rice
　　½ cup sliced, fresh green beans
　　1 (6-ounce) can tomato paste
　　1 cup water

Season the cube steaks with the salt, pepper and garlic powder. Place the sliced onion in the bottom of the pot. Place the cube steaks on top of the onions. Add the rice on top of steaks. Distribute the beans on top of the rice. Combine the water and tomato paste and pour over everything. Heat the liquid, then cover, reduce the flame to low and simmer for 30 minutes.

Suggestion: Serve the cooked cube steaks between slices of real rye bread, or as open face sandwiches, drizzling the tomato sauce over the meat

Nutritional information per serving: 849 calories (10% from fat), 9.5 g. fat, 65 g. protein, 125.7 g. carbohydrates, 128 mgs. cholesterol.

The reason chipped beef worked so well during World War II was that it could be eaten by hungry soldiers even when food preservation facilities were limited. Yes, yes we know what this was renamed during the war. Still, chipped beef offers trekkers another advantage, one overlooked for years—it's incredibly low-fat.

Bulge-Battlin' Chipped Beef

6 ounces dried beef, shredded
1 cup water
1 cup skim milk (either from powder or diluted evaporated)
2 to 3 tablespoons all-purpose flour
2 hard-boiled eggs, chilled, shells and yolks removed, whites
chopped
salt and pepper to taste

Add the water and beef to the pot, place over a medium flame and bring to a slow boil. Lower the flame and simmer for about five minutes. Remove from the flame and drain off the water. Add the milk and return to the heat. Warm, but do not boil. Slowly stir in flour to thicken sauce. Add the egg whites and season with the salt and pepper. Simmer until the eggs are heated through. Serve over a split hard roll.

Nutritional information per serving: 611 calories (13.4% from fat), 9.1 g. fat, 69 g. protein, 55 g. carbohydrates, 76 mgs. cholesterol.

What does any trekker get when combining beef and a pot over a solitary flame? Nothing less than the trans-continental complete meal.

Yankee Doodle Pot Roast

2 teaspoons canola oil
½ pound beef top round, trimmed of all visible fat
1½ cups water
2 reduced-sodium beef bouillon cubes
2 medium potatoes, peeled and quartered
2 carrots, peeled and sliced
1 large onion, peeled and cut into chunks
salt and pepper to taste

Add the oil to the pot and place over medium heat. When the oil is hot, but not smoking, add the beef and brown on all sides. Add the remaining ingredients, cover, lower the flame and gently simmer for 45 minutes or longer. Stir every once in a while to keep the beef from sticking to the bottom of the pan.

Suggestion: Hard rolls, such as Kaiser rolls, will soak up every last drop of the flavorful gravy this dish makes.

Nutritional information per serving: 856 calories (18.1% from fat), 17.2 g. fat, 64 g. protein, 111.5 g. carbohydrates, 128 mgs. cholesterol.

The pot is a miracle worker with pork. Pork has been bred leaner and leaner over the years. That's good news for healthy eaters, but has created the impression that it also has become dry. Not so in the pot. Since moisture is used to cook the pork, it stays nice and juicy.

Pam's Pork Chops

    2 ribs celery, chopped
    1 medium onion, peeled and cut into chunks
    2 carrots, peeled and cut into chunks
    1 potato, scrubbed and cut into quarters
    1 large tomato, cored and diced
    1 medium turnip, peeled and cut into chunks
    ½ teaspoon salt
    1 reduced-sodium beef bouillon cube
    1 medium bay leaf
    ¼ teaspoon dried thyme, crumbled
    ground black pepper to taste
    1½ cups water
    2 center-cut loin pork chops, trimmed of all visible fat

Add all the vegetables and seasonings to the pot, along with the water. Stir until evenly distributed. Lay the pork chops on top of the vegetables. Bring to a boil over a medium flame, then reduce the flame to low and gently simmer for one hour.

Hint: For a wonderful flavor, full of Shakespearean overtones, substitute one large leek for the onion.

Nutritional information per serving: 725 calories (15.8% from fat), 12.8 g. fat, 61 g. protein, 92.7 g. carbohydrates, 143 mgs. cholesterol.

Holy Toledo Chops

    2 teaspoons canola oil
    2 thick center-cut pork loin chops, trimmed of all visible fat (12 ounces, total)
    1 medium onion, peeled and sliced

1 medium green pepper, core and seeds removed, cut into strips
1 large potato, scrubbed and sliced
3 packets tomato ketchup
2 tablespoons molasses
2 tablespoons water

Add the oil to the pot and place over a medium flame. When the oil is hot, but not smoking, add the pork chops and cook until lightly browned on both sides. Remove the chops from the pot and carefully drain off any fat. Place the sliced onion in the bottom of the pan. Lay the chops on the onion. Distribute the remaining vegetables on top of the pork. Drizzle the ketchup, molasses and water over all. Cover, reduce the flame to low and cook for 40 minutes. Add more water if the sauce is too thick. Serves two.

Suggestion: If you've got the room, slices of whole-grain bread round out this meal very nicely.

Nutritional information per serving: 473 calories (20.8% from fat), 10.9 g. fat, 40.5 g. protein, 51.5 g. carbohydrates, 107 mgs. cholesterol.

Healthy Soup's On

Don Mauer started his soup pot at an early age. Grandmother Mauer believed that a masterfully assembled pot of soup could cure everything from cold feet to sibling rivalry.

Today, when cooking soups in his own kitchen, a large 12-quart stock pot dominates Don's stovetop. Potable, but not too portable. A one-quart kettle is about as large as it gets on the trail, unless you're into hauling some serious hardware. Plan accordingly.

For the Bottomline Soup recipe, you can combine all dry ingredients in a bag at home. On the trail, all you'll have to do is dump them into the boiling water—no need to measure.

Bottomline Soup

1 teaspoon canola oil
6 ounces lean meat to match the flavor of the bouillon (optional)
2½ cups water
3 low-sodium bouillon cubes (chicken, beef or vegetable)
1 small tomato (or 2 to 3 tablespoons tomato paste or a small
    handful of sun-dried tomatoes)
1 large carrot, chopped (or equivalent volume of freeze-dried)
1 handful freeze-dried peas
1 handful freeze-dried potatoes

½ teaspoon celery seeds
1 tablespoon dried parsley
1 tablespoon dried onion flakes
ground black pepper and garlic powder to taste

Add the oil to the pot and place over a medium flame. When the oil is hot, but not smoking, add the optional meat and cook until it loses its pink color. Add the water and bouillon cubes. Bring to a boil and add the remaining ingredients. Reduce the flame to low, cover and simmer for about 25 to 30 minutes.

Nutritional information per serving (with optional meat): 492 calories (22.5% from fat), 12.3 g. fat, 51 g. protein, 46.3 g. carbohydrates, 97 mgs. cholesterol.

Lickity Split Pea Soup

2½ cups water
¼ teaspoon salt
1 cup freeze-dried peas (or more for a thicker soup)
½ cup diced lean smoked ham
1 carrot, peeled and diced
½ teaspoon dried thyme, crumbled

Add the water and salt to the pot and place over a medium flame. Add the remaining ingredients, lower the flame, cover and gently simmer for about 45 minutes or until the peas are very soft, stirring occasionally.

Suggestion: Serve with fat-free crackers or slices of whole-grain bread.

Nutritional information per serving: 315 calories (10.9% from fat), 3.8 g. fat, 28 g. protein, 45.7 g. carbohydrates, 26 mgs. cholesterol.

The old trappers of the North Woods had it right when they made this dish. The soup has great flavor, but takes at least one hour to cook. Save it for a lazy day on your trip.

Trapper's Pea Soup

2 cups water
1 cup dried (not freeze-dried) yellow or green split peas
water
¼ teaspoon salt
1 medium onion, peeled and diced

½ **cup lean smoked ham, diced (or a smoked pork chop, trimmed
of all visible fat)**
black pepper to taste
1½ tablespoons all-purpose flour

Add the peas to the pot and cover with water. Add the salt and bring
to a boil over a medium flame, stirring to prevent sticking. Add the
ham (or pork chop) and onion. Cover, reduce the flame to low and
simmer for at least one hour, adding flour to thicken if desired. If you
used a smoked pork chop, it may be served on the side once the soup
is completed.

*Nutritional information per serving: 396 calories (8.4% from fat), 3.7 g. fat,
28 g. protein, 63 g. carbohydrates, 26 mgs. cholesterol.*

Science has finally proven that chicken soup does help a cold.
We've noticed that it also can lift your spirits. Once the fat has been
skimmed from the top of traditional chicken soup, it is even
healthier. What more can you ask from a simple soup?

"Usin' Your Noodle" Soup

2½ cups water
½ teaspoon salt
½ whole chicken breast, skin removed
2 carrots, diced
1 tablespoon onion flakes
ground black pepper to taste
1 medium bay leaf
¼ teaspoon dried thyme, crumbled
½ cup dry medium noodles

Add the water, salt and chicken to the pot. Place over a medium flame
and bring to a boil. Lower the flame and gently simmer until the meat
falls off the bone, about 45 minutes. Remove the bones, add the
remaining ingredients, except for the noodles. Add additional water if
necessary. Cook for another 25 minutes, or until the carrots are cooked.
Add the noodles and cook for seven to ten minutes more.

*Nutritional information per serving: 397 calories (5.9% from fat), 2.6 g. fat,
36 g. protein, 55.6 g. carbohydrates, 68 mgs. cholesterol.*

We've always been a bit chicken when it comes to building a meal out of soup...especially when it's been stewing for a while.

Little Rhody Stew

   2½ cups water
   8 ounces cooked chicken breast meat only, cut into chunks
   3 reduced-sodium chicken bouillon cubes
   2 potatoes, peeled and diced
   1 carrot, peeled and chopped
   1 medium onion, peeled and chopped
   ¼ teaspoon cayenne pepper
   1 clove garlic, skin removed and crushed
   ¼ teaspoon black pepper
   1 small tomato, cored and quartered
   ½ cup dried corn kernels

Place all the ingredients, except the tomato and corn, in the pot. Place over a medium flame and bring to a boil. Cover, lower the flame, and gently simmer for 30 minutes. Add the tomato and corn, and simmer for 15 minutes more. Add water as needed. Thicken with flour if needed.

Nutritional information per serving: 892 calories (5% from fat), 5 g. fat, 77 g. protein, 136.2 g. carbohydrates, 136 mgs. cholesterol.

A lean piece of steak can be turned into a very tasty stew. This stew has a rich flavor, yet is easy to prepare. Ahh, the virtues of the pot out on the trail!

Steak Stew with Dandy Dumplings

   1 cup all-purpose flour
   ½ pound top round, trimmed of all visible fat and cut into cubes
   2½ teaspoons canola oil
   2 cups water
   2 medium potatoes, scrubbed and cubed
   1 medium onion, peeled and cut into chunks
   2 carrots, scrubbed and cut into chunks
   salt and pepper to taste
   1 medium bay leaf
   1 teaspoon Worcestershire sauce
   celery seed, to taste
   ¼ cup nonfat egg substitute

Place the flour in a bowl and dredge the steak in the flour. Set the remaining flour aside. Add the oil to the pot and place over a medium flame. When hot, but not smoking, add the beef and brown, turning to prevent sticking. Add the water and scrape the pot's bottom with a spoon.

Add the remaining ingredients, cover and simmer for 30 minutes, stirring occasionally.

Add a little water, a dash of canola oil and the nonfat egg substitute to the remaining flour. Mix into a sticky dough.With an oiled spoon, drop balls of the dough onto the stew, cover the pot, lower the flame and simmer for five minutes.

Nutritional information per serving: 653 calories (13.9% fat), 10 g. fat, 40 g. protein, 99 g. carbohydrates, 64 mgs. cholesterol

---

Northland Corn Chowder

4 ounces cooked chicken breast meat only, chopped
2 cups water
½ cup dried corn
¼ cup onion flakes
1 rib celery, chopped
1 packet dried nonfat milk (one-quart size or 1⅓ cups)
salt and pepper to taste
2 to 3 tablespoons all-purpose flour (optional)

Add all of the ingredients, except the flour, to the pot. Place over a medium flame and cook until the corn is rehydrated. If thickening is needed, mix flour with a few tablespoons of water to make a paste. Stir well while adding the paste to the chowder to prevent lumping. Cook briefly until the chowder thickens.

Nutritional information per serving (without the optional flour): 656 calories (6% from fat), 4.4 g. fat, 63 g. protein, 90.5 g. carbohydrates, 84 mgs. cholesterol.

Vegetables

Vegetables do just as well in the pot as meat, and the beauty is in their low fat content. Seasoned just right, vegetables have plenty of flavor. Most of the time, they end up on the side. However, you can make up some exciting veggie combos that can stand alone as a main dish.

Borderland Spuds

1 teaspoon canola oil
6 ounces Canadian bacon, diced
1 medium onion, peeled and chopped
1 medium sweet green pepper, cored, seeded and chopped
1 rib celery, chopped
2 large potatoes, scrubbed and sliced
¼ cup fresh parsley, chopped

Add the oil to the pot and place over a medium flame. When the oil is hot, but not smoking, add the bacon and stir until lightly browned. Add the onions, peppers and celery. Sauté until tender. Add the potatoes, stir, reduce the flame and cover. Stir occasionally. After 30 minutes, add the parsley. Cook until the potatoes start to fall apart.

Nutritional information per serving: 853 calories (18.5% from fat), 17.5 g. fat, 47 g. protein, 128 g. carbohydrates, 84 mgs. cholesterol.

"Hey, Tomata" Lunch

2 cups water
3 large tomatoes
¼ cup water
1 sweet green pepper, diced
1 medium onion, peeled and diced
2 tablespoons granulated sugar
salt and pepper to taste
½ cup uncooked instant rice

Add the two cups of water to the pot and place over a high flame. When the water boils, scald the tomatoes by dipping them in the water for 30 seconds, using a slotted spoon. Remove the tomatoes from the water. Allow the tomatoes to cool till they can be handled, and carefully (they'll still be hot) peel and core. Empty the water from the pot. Return the tomatoes to the pot and add the quarter-cup of water. Cover, reduce the flame to low, and simmer for 20 minutes. Add the remaining ingredients and cook for another ten to 15 minutes, stirring to prevent sticking.

Nutritional information per serving: 619 calories (3.2% from fat), 2.2 g. fat, 11 g. protein, 141.3 g. carbohydrates, no cholesterol.

Tasty Tater Salad

2 cups water
2 large potatoes, peeled and cut into quarters
3 hard-boiled eggs, whites only
¼ cup diced green onion
3 tablespoons nonfat salad dressing (such as Miracle Whip®)
1 tablespoon yellow mustard
salt and pepper to taste

Add the water and potatoes to the pot. Place over a medium flame, bring to a boil, cover and cook for 25 minutes. Drain, cool and cut the potatoes into small chunks. Dice the egg whites. Return the potatoes and egg whites to the cooled pot and add the remaining ingredients. Stir and toss until well combined and coated with the dressing. Serve.

Nutritional information per serving: 536 calories (2.4% from fat), 1.4 g. fat, 18 g. protein, 113.2 g. carbohydrates, no cholesterol.

Linguine is very similar to spaghetti, except it's flatter and not round. It's the perfect pasta for this cool salad. If you don't have linguine, any long thin pasta will do.

Linger A While Over This Linguine

½ pound dry linguine pasta
water
1 teaspoon peanut oil
1 teaspoon minced fresh ginger root
1 tablespoon granulated sugar
2 tablespoons fat-reduced creamy-style peanut butter
2 tablespoons sodium-reduced soy sauce
1 tablespoon white wine vinegar
¼ teaspoon crushed red pepper flakes (more if you like it spicy)
2 scallions, cut on the diagonal into one-inch pieces

Fill the pot two-thirds of the way to the top with water and place over a high flame. When the water boils, add the linguine and cook according to package directions, usually ten to 12 minutes.

Drain the water and toss the pasta in the pot with the oil. Set aside to cool. In a small bowl, using a wire whisk, whisk together the remaining ingredients, except for the scallion, until completely combined. Pour the sauce over the cooled linguine and toss till coated. Sprinkle the scallions over the top. Serves two.

Nutritional information per serving: 578 calories (18.8% from fat), 12 g. fat, 20 g. protein, 98.3 g. carbohydrates, no cholesterol.

Just Desserts

Remember the fifth grade, when your teacher made Indian Pudding in early October? Through the mists of memory, the wonderful aroma rising from that pot held great promise. Well, this Indian Pudding delivers all that flavor, is easy to prepare and will put a marvelous low-fat topper on a great meal.

Indian Corn Pudding

  1 (8 ounce) can fat-free, sweetened, condensed milk
  ½ cup water
  3 tablespoons diet margarine
  3 tablespoons brown sugar
  ½ teaspoon ground nutmeg
  ½ teaspoon ground cinnamon
  ½ cup nonfat egg substitute
  ¾ cup yellow cornmeal
  ¼ cup seedless raisins

Add the condensed milk and water to the pot, place over a low flame and bring to a gentle simmer. Add the margarine, sugar and spices. Once the sugar is dissolved, add the egg substitute, cornmeal and raisins. Stir, cover and cook over a low flame for ten minutes. Stir often to keep from sticking. Serves four.

Nutritional information per serving: 457 calories (4.3% from fat), 2.2 g. fat, 13 g. protein, 95 g. carbohydrates, 10 mgs. cholesterol.

This next recipe isn't some spooky Halloween dessert. The orange referred to in the name is not about the pudding's color, but rather the flavor. Start this dessert before dinner. By the time the main course is prepared, served and eaten, the pudding will be ready.

Fresh Orange Pudding

  2 oranges, peeled and sliced
  1 teaspoon granulated sugar
  ⅔ cup skim milk (prepared from instant)
  1 egg yolk
  pinch salt
  1 tablespoon cornstarch
  1½ tablespoons granulated sugar

Put the oranges in a heat-proof bowl and sprinkle the teaspoon of sugar over them. Add the milk, egg yolk, salt, cornstarch and sugar to the pot. Place over a medium flame and stir until combined. When it begins to thicken, pour over the orange slices. Allow to cool.

Nutritional information per serving: 367 calories (14.7% from fat), 6 g. fat, 10 g. protein, 72.4 g. carbohydrates, 216 mgs. cholesterol.

Don't Trifle with Me

Trifle base:
 ¾ cup sliced fresh strawberries (blueberries are great, too)
 1 tablespoon granulated sugar.
 2 reduced-fat Twinkies®, sliced the long way
Custard ingredients:
 1 cup skim milk
 ¼ cup nonfat egg substitute
 2 tablespoons granulated sugar
 1 tablespoon cornstarch

Add the strawberries to a bowl and sprinkle with the sugar. Place the sliced Twinkies on top, not over-lapping. Set aside.

Add the custard ingredients to the pot and place over a medium flame. Stir constantly until the custard thickens, but do not boil. Pour the custard over the fruit/Twinkie mixture. Allow to cool. Serves two.

Nutritional information per serving: 448 calories (3.7% from fat), 1.9 g. fat, 26.5 g. protein, 59.7 g. carbohydrates, 12 mgs. cholesterol.

Jonathan's Sauce

This applesauce tastes great with store-bought, fat-free oatmeal raisin cookies, or add a handful of seedless raisins.
 ¼ cup water
 3 apples, peeled, cored and cut into chunks
 2 tablespoons brown sugar
 ½ teaspoon ground cinnamon
 ¼ teaspoon ground nutmeg

Add the water and apples to the pot and place over a medium flame. When the water begins to boil, lower the flame, cover and gently simmer until the apples fall apart. Remove from the flame, add the sugar and spices and stir well till sauce consistency.

Nutritional information per serving: 289 calories (4% from fat), 1.3 g. fat, trace of protein, 75.5 g. carbohydrates, no cholesterol.

Steaming vegetables, since it preserves all the good nutrients, has been in vogue for years. Your pot is great for steaming anything, but especially for fruit.

Steamy Apple Amusement

2 Macintosh apples, top half peeled
1 tablespoon granulated sugar
2 tablespoons seedless raisins
½ teaspoon ground cinnamon
water

Core the apples without puncturing the bottom of the fruit (a melon baller is the perfect tool).

In a bowl, stir together the sugar and raisins. Stuff the pocket of each apple with the raisin/sugar mix. Sprinkle the cinnamon over the top of the apples. Place the steamer basket in the pot and add enough water to reach the bottom of the steamer. Place the apples on the steamer, cover and place the pot over a medium flame. When steam begins to come from under the pot's cover, lower the flame and steam for 30 minutes, adding water if needed.

Suggestion: You can prepare this recipe with pears, as well. Choose two Bosc pears (they're perfect for steaming). Use two tablespoons of dried apricots, chopped, in place of the raisins and top with a light sprinkle of chopped fresh mint leaves instead of cinnamon. The pears should steam for about the same time.

Nutritional information per serving: *263 calories (4.1% from fat), 1.2 g. fat, 1 g. protein, 69 g. carbohydrates, no cholesterol.*

Remarkable Rice Dessert

½ cup water
½ cup raw long-grain white rice
½ cup seedless raisins
1 apple, peeled, cored and sliced
1 tablespoon brown sugar
½ teaspoon ground cinnamon
¼ teaspoon ground nutmeg

Add the water and rice to the pot. Place over a medium flame and bring to a boil. Stir in the raisins and apple. Cover, lower the flame, and cook about 15 minutes, or until rice is tender. Remove the pot from the flame and stir in the remaining ingredients. Set aside for ten minutes to cool. If you wish, add a little milk and more sugar. Serves two.

Nutritional information per serving *(without additional milk or sugar): 334 calories (1.9% from fat), 0.7 g. fat, 4.5 g. protein, 80.7 g. carbohydrates, no cholesterol.*

One of DJ's favorite desserts from the pot is fruit compote. All the ingredients are easy to bring to the campsite and the compote is ready a few short minutes. Big plus: It has zero added fat.

DJ's Fruity 'pote

½ cup dried apricots
½ cup seedless raisins
1 (6-ounce) can Mandarin orange segments
1 fresh peach, peeled and quartered, pit discarded
3 tablespoons granulated sugar
⅓ cup water

Add all of the ingredients to the pot and place over a medium flame. Stir until the sugar dissolves. When the water begins to boil, lower the flame and cover the pot. Cook, stirring frequently, for about 20 minutes. Add water, if needed. Serves two.

Suggestion: Serve over a slice of store-bought, fat-free pound cake.

Nutritional information per serving: *323 calories (1.3% from fat), 0.5 g. fat, 4 g. protein, 84.7 g. carbohydrates, no cholesterol.*

THE OVEN

There is nothing to compare with the adventures of cooking in an oven outside. The meals are tasty and easy. On the other hand, an oven will make you work for your dinner (or breakfast).

We discussed the merits of various types of ovens in Chapter Three. Whatever oven you decide to use—homemade, Outback®, Mirro®, BakePacker® or other—be sure you know the benefits and limitations of each. Following the directions that come with the oven is important. It just wouldn't do to expect a casserole with browned bread crumbs if the oven you're packing cooks with steam. Also, make sure the oven pan is of a non-stick variety to cut down on the oil needed to prepare these recipes.

As with all trekking utensils, you have to exercise a little care when using an oven. Holding the "bake" line on an Outback Oven requires deft command of the heat control on most one-burner stoves. If you master the skills, however, the cobbler you bake will be great, the quiche exciting and the bird brilliant.

Rise And Shine With Your Oven

It sounds a bit European, but the oven does open up continental cuisine for the patient outdoor chef.

Quiche is a mouth-watering French pie known for its great flavor and high fat content. How do we get around that problem?

Bisquick® has marketed a low-fat version of its famous mix, which can be used to make an acceptable pie crust. A couple of leaner substitutions for the quiche's contents—et voilá, a low-fat quiche any Frenchman would be proud of.

One Pan Gourmet Lite Quiche

1 cup Bisquick® reduced-fat baking mix
6 tablespoons water
¼ cup grated nonfat cheddar cheese
⅓ cup diced 98%-lean ham
⅓ cup evaporated skim milk
½ cup nonfat egg substitute
salt and pepper to taste

Begin heating the oven to medium. Add the baking mix and water to the non-stick oven pan and stir until combined. Smooth out with the back of the spoon so that it is level. Sprinkle the cheese over the batter and distribute the ham on top of the cheese. Beat the milk, nonfat egg substitute, salt and pepper together and pour over ham and cheese. Place pan in the oven on the lower rack for 20 minutes, or until the filling is firm. Remove from the oven. Cut the quiche into wedges and serve.

Nutritional information per serving: 735 calories (13.5% from fat), 11 g. fat, 45 g. protein, 107.4 g. carbohydrates, 29 mgs. cholesterol.

While not exactly upper crust, this next taste-tempter will get your battery charged and help keep the doctor away for at least two days!

Eggy Apples

2 medium apples (Macintosh work well)
4 ounces reduced-fat breakfast sausage
½ cup nonfat egg substitute
salt and pepper to taste

Begin heating the oven to medium.Core the apples from the top, making certain to not break through the bottom. Use a spoon to hollow out the inside of the apple to make a pocket. In the process, widen the opening at the top. Fill the apples about two-thirds full with the sausage and place in the non-stick oven pan. Pour the egg substitute over the sausage in the pocket of the apple. Sprinkle with salt and pepper. Bake for 25 to 30 minutes.

Nutritional information per serving: 462 calories (33.8% from fat), 17.4 g. fat, 28 g. protein, 48 g. carbohydrates, 64 mgs. cholesterol.

This is a low-fat scrambled version of an old favorite from the cantons in the Old Country.

Swiss Family Robinson's Eggs

1 tablespoon diet margarine
⅓ cup grated reduced-fat Swiss cheese
¼ cup evaporated skim milk
½ cup nonfat egg substitute

Add the margarine to the non-stick oven pan and place over a medium flame to melt. Sprinkle about three-quarters of the cheese on the bottom of the pan. Pour the nonfat egg substitute onto the cheese. Pour the milk over the egg substitute and sprinkle the remaining cheese on top. Place in the oven for 20 minutes, maximum.

Suggestion: Serve with a hard roll and fresh fruit. The additions will boost the meal's calories and bring calories coming from fat to 20%.) This is a recipe determined to stay with you in one way or another for the whole day!

Nutritional information per serving: 229 calories (33% from fat), 8.4 g. fat, 27 g. protein, 9.2 g. carbohydrates, 2 mgs. cholesterol.

Caribe Egg-on

1 medium Bermuda onion
½ cup nonfat egg substitute
¼ teaspoon dried tarragon, crumbled
1 tablespoon grated Parmesan cheese
2 tablespoon fresh or dried parsley, chopped
2 tablespoons bread crumbs
fresh ground black pepper to taste

Begin heating the oven to medium.

Cut the onion in half along the "equator" (with the stem and root being the poles). With a spoon, scoop out the inner rings of the onion, creating two cups. Place the onion cups in the oven pan and divide the nonfat egg substitute between the two halves. Dice the remaining onion and sprinkle on top. Combine the cheese, parsley, bread crumbs and pepper. Place a healthy scoop on top of the diced onions. Gently smooth to cover entire cavity, adding extra as needed. Bake for about 15 minutes or until the bread crumbs are browned.

Suggestion: For added flavor, sprinkle some diced lean ham in the oven pan before cooking.

Nutritional information per serving: 217 calories (10.4% from fat), 2.5 g. fat, 16 g. protein, 29.2 g. carbohydrates, 4 mgs. cholesterol.

Dutchman's Wundercake

2 tablespoons diet margarine
2 tablespoons dark brown sugar
1 large apple, peeled, cored and sliced lengthwise into eighth-inch thick slices

⅛ teaspoon ground cinnamon
¼ cup nonfat egg substitute
¼ cup skim milk
⅓ cup Bisquick® reduced-fat baking mix

Begin heating the oven to medium. Add the margarine to the non-stick oven pan and place in the oven until the margarine melts. Carefully remove the pan from the oven and spread the brown sugar evenly on the bottom of the pan. Lay the apple slices evenly on the sugar. Sprinkle the cinnamon over the apple.

In a bowl or large cup, stir together the remaining ingredients and pour the batter over the fruit and sugar. Bake for about 20 minutes, or until the top of the cake is nicely browned. Flip the cake out onto a plate so the brown sugar and apples are on top.

Nutritional information per serving: 379 calories (16.4% from fat), 6.9 g. fat, 11 g. protein, 68.2 g. carbohydrates, 1 mgs. cholesterol.

Thunder Bay Special

1 teaspoon canola oil
6 slices Canadian bacon
½ cup nonfat egg substitute
½ cup skim milk
½ teaspoon granulated sugar
½ cup all-purpose flour
½ cup white cornmeal
1 teaspoon baking powder
fresh ground black pepper to taste

Begin heating the oven to medium.

Add the canola oil to the non-stick oven pan and place over a medium flame. When the oil is hot, but not smoking, cook the Canadian bacon until lightly browned. Drain off any excess grease and oil. While the bacon is cooking, stir together the nonfat egg substitute and milk in a bowl until combined. Add the sugar, flour, baking powder and corn-meal, and stir until just moistened, about 20 to 30 seconds. Once the bacon is cooked, pour the batter over it and place the pan in the hot oven for ten minutes. Reduce the heat to low and continue baking until the cake is set in the center. Serves two.

Nutritional information per serving: 447 calories (18.6% from fat), 9.3 g. fat, 32 g. protein, 57.1 g. carbohydrates, 43 mgs. cholesterol.

Lunch and Dinner, Oven-Style

Light up your campsite. Amaze your friends. Use your One Pan expertise to turn your outdoor kitchen into a full service eatery. From roasts and casseroles to pies, cakes and bread, as well as snacks and pizza for color, the oven is a great trailside companion.

Of Chicken and Other Fowl Things

Chicken breast is one of the leanest meats to cook in the oven. Here's one of the easiest ways to bake a chicken breast.

"Don't Beat Your Breast" Basic Chicken

1 whole skinless, boneless chicken breast, split
1 medium onion, sliced
1 rib of celery, chopped
1 medium carrot, cut into strips
1 medium potato, cleaned and cut into chunks
salt and black pepper to taste

Begin heating the oven to medium. Place the chicken in the non-stick oven pan and surround with the vegetables. Sprinkle with the salt and pepper. Bake for about 40 minutes. Serve with a hard roll and fresh fruit.

Nutritional information per serving: 532 calories (5.8% from fat), 3.4 g. fat, 59 g. protein, 62.7 g. carbohydrates, 136 mgs. cholesterol.

Blue Plate Chicken

1 whole chicken breast, skinned, boned and split
**1 cup precooked wild and white rice combination (Uncle Ben's®
or Rice-A-Roni®, etc.)**
1 sweet red pepper, cored and cut into strips
1 sweet green pepper, cored and cut into strips
1 carrot, peeled and cut into strips

Begin heating the oven to medium. Place the chicken breasts in the non-stick oven pan and surround with the pre-cooked rice mixture. Lay the pepper and carrot strips over the top of the chicken. Cover and bake for 35 to 45 minutes, or until the chicken is cooked through.

Nutritional information per serving: 487 calories (6.8% from fat), 3.7 g. fat, 61 g. protein, 49.7 g. carbohydrates, 136 mgs. cholesterol.

Want to put an edge on your dinner? Add a couple of shots of hot sauce to the next recipe.

KC's BBQ'd Bird

1 reduced-sodium beef bouillon cube
½ cup hot water
1 tomato, cored and crushed
1 tablespoon Worcestershire sauce
4 tablespoons tomato ketchup
1 medium onion, diced
¼ teaspoon dry mustard
1 teaspoon dried parsley leaves
¼ teaspoon salt
¼ teaspoon ground black pepper
1 whole skinless, boneless chicken breast, split
1 cup precooked white or brown rice

Start heating the oven to medium. In a bowl, dissolve the bouillon cube in hot water. Stir in the remaining ingredients except for the chicken and rice. Place the chicken breasts in the non-stick oven pan and pour the sauce over all. Bake for 35 minutes. Add the rice to the pan and bake ten minutes more.

Nutritional information per serving: *641 calories (6.5% from fat), 4.6 g. fat, 60 g. protein, 84.8 g. carbohydrates, 136 mgs. cholesterol.*

Brought along a special wine for Saturday night? Super. The following goes great with a Marsane or Riesling.

Chicken Dijonaise

1 whole chicken breast, skinned, boned and split
1 clove garlic, minced
2 tablespoons Dijon-style mustard
¼ teaspoon dried thyme leaves, crumbled
salt and pepper to taste

Begin heating the oven to high. Rinse the chicken and pat dry. Mix the garlic with the mustard, thyme, salt and pepper. Rub the mustard mixture on the meat. Place the chicken breasts in the non-stick oven pan and bake 35 to 40 minutes on the low rack (medium bake in the Outback Oven).

Suggestion: Cut a baking potato in half, wrap in foil and bake on the higher rack while the chicken bakes on the lower rack.

Nutritional information per serving: 301 calories (15% from fat), 5 g. fat, 54 g. protein, 1.2 g. carbohydrates, 136 mgs. cholesterol.

This-Can't-Be-Chicken Chicken

1 lemon
1 tablespoon dried mustard
1 teaspoon light brown sugar
½ teaspoon ground coriander
¼ teaspoon ground black pepper
1 whole chicken breast, skinned, boned and split
¾ cup seedless raisins
1 cup precooked noodles

Begin heating the oven to medium/high.

Squeeze the lemon into a cup or bowl. Dice about one tablespoon of the lemon peel, adding it and the dry seasonings to the bowl. Stir until combined. Place the chicken in the non-stick oven pan and place the pan on the lower oven rack. Bake for 15 minutes. Carefully remove the pan from the oven. Turn the chicken breasts over and spoon half the sauce mixture over the chicken. Return the pan to the oven and bake 15 minutes more. Carefully remove the pan from the oven, add the raisins and the balance of the sauce to the pan. Bake for 15 minutes. Serve with precooked noodles (which can be heated by wrapping in foil and warming for five minutes on top rack of the oven).

Nutritional information per serving: 860 calories (8% from fat), 7.6 g. fat, 68 g. protein, 138 g carbohydrates, 136 mgs. cholesterol.

Big Kahuna Potted Chicken

1 teaspoon olive oil
2 tablespoons diced sweet green pepper
1 small onion, sliced
¼ cup sliced mushrooms
2 tablespoons all-purpose flour
¾ cup skim milk (prepared from instant)
¼ cup nonfat egg substitute
1 tablespoon thin sliced pimento
ground black pepper to taste
1 pre-cooked skinless boneless chicken breast, diced
2 tablespoons bread crumbs

Heat the oven to medium. Add the oil to the non-stick oven pan and place over a medium flame. Add the green pepper, onion and mushrooms. Add the flour and blend. Stir in the milk, nonfat egg substitute, pimento and pepper, cooking until thickened. Add the chicken. Stir and remove from the flame. Cover with a layer of bread crumbs and bake for 25 minutes or until the bread crumbs are browned.

Nutritional information per serving: 580 calories (13.8% from fat), 8.9 g. fat, 69 g. protein, 47.7 g. carbohydrates, 139 mgs. cholesterol.

Squashed Fowl

½ cup seasoned bread crumbs
¼ cup shredded Parmesan cheese
1 yellow or zucchini squash, cleaned, trimmed and cut into one-inch thick slices
¼ cup skim milk (prepared from instant)
1 whole chicken breast, skinned, boned and split

Begin heating the oven to medium.

On a plate, mix together the bread crumbs and cheese. Dip the chicken in the milk and roll in the crumb mixture. Place the coated chicken in the non-stick oven pan. Dip the squash in the milk and then the crumb mixture. Arrange the squash on top of the chicken. Bake for 45 minutes.

Nutritional information per serving: 631 calories (17.3% from fat), 12.1 g. fat, 74 g. protein, 53.4 g. carbohydrates, 153 mgs. cholesterol.

Corny Clucker Pot Pie

1 (1-ounce) packet chicken gravy mix
1 (8.5-ounce) package instant corn muffin mix (the Jiffy brand works well)
¼ cup nonfat egg substitute
⅓ cup skim milk
1 pre-cooked chicken breast, skinned, boned and diced
1 carrot, peeled and diced
1 potato, sliced thin
1 rib celery, strings removed and diced

Over a medium to low flame, prepare the gravy mix in a cup per packet directions. Set aside.

Add the corn muffin mix, nonfat egg substitute and milk to a bowl. Stir together until combined. Set aside. Begin heating the oven to medium.

Mix the chicken and vegetables together in the non-stick oven pan. Pour the prepared gravy over the chicken and vegetables and stir to mix. Pour the corn bread batter over all and smooth out to the edge of the pan. Bake in a medium oven for 20 to 25 minutes or until the corn bread is lightly browned. Serves two.

Nutritional information per serving: 804 calories (18.5% from fat), 16.5 g. fat, 44.5 g. protein, 116 g. carbohydrates, 72 mgs. cholesterol.

Philly Chicken

½ cup skim milk (prepared from instant)
½ cup reduced-fat cheddar cheese, shredded
1 pre-cooked chicken breast, skinned, boned and diced
1 cup pre-cooked macaroni
1 sweet red pepper, core removed and diced
2 tablespoons seasoned bread crumbs

Over a medium flame, heat the milk to almost boiling. Add the cheese and stir until smooth.

Begin heating the oven to medium. In the non-stick oven pan, combine the chicken, macaroni and red pepper. Pour the cheese sauce over the top. Sprinkle a layer of bread crumbs over all. Bake for 25 minutes.

Nutritional information per serving: 741 calories (18.3% from fat), 15.1 g. fat, 85 g. protein, 61.3 g. carbohydrates, 138 mgs. cholesterol.

Lanai's Classy Chicken

1 whole chicken breast, split, skinned and boned
⅓ cup rehydrated freeze-dried green beans
1 orange, peeled and sliced across the grain into rounds
1 small can of juice-packed crushed pineapple
¼ teaspoon ground ginger
¼ teaspoon ground cinnamon
½ cup pre-cooked white or brown rice

Begin heating the oven to medium/high.

Place the chicken breasts in the non-stick oven pan. Surround with the - green beans. Lay the orange slices over the top and pour the crushed pineapple, including juice, over all. Sprinkle with the ginger and cinnamon and cover with foil (not needed with the Outback Oven). Bake for 45 minutes. (If baked on the upper rack, use higher flame.)

If there's room in the pan, add the rice five minutes before serving. If not, remove the chicken pan from the oven at the proper time. Wrap the rice in foil and cook on top rack for five minutes, or until heated.

Nutritional information per serving: 506 calories (6.4% from fat), 3.6 g. fat, 58 g. protein, 58.7 g. carbohydrates, 136 mgs. cholesterol.

Mrs. Bead's Bird

1 whole chicken breast, split, skinned and boned
1 cup broccoli florets
1 packet Lipton Cup-A-Soup® mushroom soup mix, reconstituted

Begin heating the oven to medium. Place the chicken breasts in the non-stick oven pan. Lay the broccoli on top. Pour the mushroom soup over all. Cover and bake for 35 to 40 minutes.

Nutritional information per serving: 355 calories (16.7% from fat), 6.6 g. fat, 57.3 g. protein, 13.7 g. carbohydrates, 136 mgs. cholesterol.

Vegetables and Pizza

Most of us have an image of the oven as the province of roasted meats. But the oven offers exciting alternatives when it comes to cooking lite.

Vegetables have long been at the center of the human diet. Their delicate flavors and wonderful textures contribute to some toothsome trail-side eating.

Seminary Souffle

1 tablespoon lite butter or diet margarine, softened
1 tablespoon all-purpose flour
3/4 cup freeze-dried corn, rehydrated (or the equivalent in
  drained canned corn)
1 cup hot skim milk
1/2 teaspoon salt
2 eggs, yolks and whites separated
ground black pepper and sweet paprika to taste

Begin heating the oven to medium-hot.

In the non-stick oven pan, blend together the butter and flour. Stir in the corn, milk and salt. In a cup, beat the egg yolks until light and add to mixture. In a clean bowl, with a wire whisk, whisk the egg whites until stiff and fold into the mixture. Add spices. Bake for about one hour.

Nutritional information per serving: 428 calories (28.8% from fat), 13.7 g. fat, 25 g. protein, 53.1 g. carbohydrates, 430 mgs. cholesterol.

Here's a recipe designed for the Outback Oven.

The One Pan Gourmet Lite Pizza

1 package instant pizza crust mix (the Gold Medal brand works well)
2 teaspoons olive oil
1 large tomato, core removed and the meat chopped
¼ cup sliced mushrooms
salt to taste
½ teaspoon dried oregano, crumbled
½ teaspoon dried basil, crumbled
½ cup reduced-fat mozzarella cheese, shredded

Begin heating the oven to high.

Prepare the pizza dough according to package directions. Flatten the dough into a 10-inch disk. With the back of a spoon, spread the olive oil over the dough surface. Sprinkle with the tomatoes and top with the mushrooms. Sprinkle with the salt and spices. Evenly distribute the cheese over all. Bake in the oven for about ten to 15 minutes, or until the crust is browned and the cheese is bubbly.

Suggestion: If pizza isn't pizza without meat, add some precooked chicken breast or 95%-lean ground beef before topping with the cheese.

Nutritional information per serving: 885 calories (22.7% from fat), 22.4 g. fat, 33 g. protein, 147.5 g. carbohydrates, 16 mgs. cholesterol.

Fortified Johnny-Cake

¼ cup all-purpose flour
1½ cups water
½ cup raw pearl barley
1 medium onion, peeled and diced
1 medium zucchini squash, trimmed and diced
½ tablespoon olive oil
¼ teaspoon salt
¼ teaspoon ground black pepper
¼ teaspoon dried oregano, crumbled

Begin heating the oven to medium.

In the non-stick oven pan, mix the flour with three-quarters of a cup of the water; stirring until smooth. Add the remaining ingredients, including the remaining three-quarters of a cup of water, stirring until combined. Bake for 30 minutes or until the water is absorbed and the top is firm.

Nutritional information per serving: 613 calories (12.2% from fat), 8.3 g. fat, 15 g. protein, 121.3 g. carbohydrates, no cholesterol.

New Way Macaroni and Cheese

½ cup skim milk (prepared from instant)
1½ cups pre-cooked macaroni
¾ cup (3 ounces) reduced-fat Monterey Jack or cheddar cheese, shredded
⅓ cup seasoned bread crumbs

Place the non-stick oven pan over a low flame and begin heating the milk. When steam begins to appear, add a half-cup of the cheese and stir until melted. Remove from the flame. Stir in the macaroni until coated with the sauce. Sprinkle the remaining cheese over all. Top with the bread crumbs. Bake for 25 to 30 minutes or until the bread crumbs are toasty brown.

Nutritional information per serving: 726 calories (23% from fat), 18.7 g. fat, 45 g. protein, 92.1 g. carbohydrates, 77 mgs. cholesterol.

Vegetable Lasagna

1 small to medium eggplant
salt
¼ cup nonfat egg substitute
¼ cup skim milk
1 tablespoon olive oil
½ cup seasoned bread crumbs
1 cup fat-free spaghetti sauce
8 ounces fat-free mozzarella cheese, shredded

Remove the ends from the eggplant and slice into quarter-inch disks (about eight to ten disks for the Outback Oven, about five disks if using a homemade oven). Sprinkle the disks with salt and set aside on a towel to drain for ten minutes. Then rinse.

While the eggplant sits, add the milk and nonfat egg substitute to a cup and stir together until combined. Set aside.

Begin heating the oil in the non-stick oven pan over a medium flame. Dip each eggplant disk in the egg mixture and then into bread crumbs. Add the eggplant to the pan and cook until lightly browned on both sides, about four to five minutes. Set aside on a paper towel to drain. Carefully dispose of any remaining oil.

Heat the oven to medium. In the non-stick oven pan, build the lasagna as follows: eggplant, then sauce, then cheese, then eggplant, etc. Make between two to four stacks. Bake for 25 to 30 minutes.

Nutritional information per serving: 797 calories (9% from fat), 8 g. fat, 89 g. protein, 88.8 g. carbohydrates, 32 mgs. cholesterol.

Ham 'n Cheese Spuds

3 medium potatoes, sliced thin
4 ounces 98%-lean ham slices, diced
⅓ cup reduced-fat cheddar cheese, grated
1 medium onion, sliced thin
¾ cup skim milk (prepared from instant)
2 tablespoons all-purpose flour
salt and pepper to taste

Begin heating the oven to medium. In the non-stick oven pan, layer the potatoes with the ham, cheese and onion. In a small bowl, stir together the milk, flour, salt and pepper. Pour the mixture over the ham, cheese and potatoes. Bake for 45 minutes.

Nutritional information per serving: 755 calories (14.3% from fat), 12 g. fat, 49 g. protein, 111.4 g. carbohydrates, 55 mgs. cholesterol.

Mushroom Stuffed Peppers

2 medium sweet green peppers
¾ cup sliced mushrooms
1 medium tomato, cored and the meat chopped
½ cup reduced-fat mozzarella cheese, grated
½ teaspoon dried oregano, crumbled
¼ teaspoon fennel seed
2 tablespoons bread crumbs

Begin heating the oven to medium. Cut the tops off the peppers and clean out the seeds. In a bowl, combine the mushrooms, tomato, cheese, oregano and fennel and stuff the peppers with the mixture. Sprinkle the bread crumbs over the top and bake for 30 to 45 minutes. Control the heat carefully by adjusting the flame, since the lower rack may need to be used due to the pepper's height.

Nutritional information per serving: 287 calories (21.3% from fat), 6.8 g. fat, 21 g. protein, 36.3 g. carbohydrates, 20 mgs. cholesterol.

If you can stuff peppers with mushrooms, you can also stuff mushrooms with all sorts of good things. Onions, spinach and a dash of Parmesan cheese give these stuffed mushrooms a terrific flavor. You won't miss the meat here for a single moment.

Square Meal Mushrooms

    4 to 6 very large mushrooms (often sold as stuffing mushrooms)
    1 small onion, minced
    ¼ cup fresh spinach leaves, stems removed and leaves minced
    1 teaspoon olive oil
    ½ teaspoon dried basil, crumbled
    ¼ teaspoon salt
    ¼ teaspoon ground black pepper
    1 tablespoon grated Parmesan cheese
    2 tablespoons bread crumbs

Begin heating the oven to high. Remove the stems from the mushrooms. Mince the stems and combine with the remaining ingredients. If the mixture does not stick together well, add more bread crumbs. Stuff each cap cavity tightly, leaving a mound a quarter-inch or so above the edge of each cap. Place the mushrooms, stuffed side up, in the non-stick oven pan and bake for ten minutes or until the stuffing begins to brown.

Nutritional information per serving: 245 calories (30.1% from fat), 8.2 g. fat, 5 g. protein, 34.1 g. carbohydrates, 4 mgs. cholesterol.

Tomatoes and 'Chokes

    1 large tomato
    2 water-packed artichoke hearts
    1 teaspoon olive oil
    3 tablespoons seasoned bread crumbs
    2 slices fat-free mozzarella cheese
    2 jumbo pimento-stuffed green olives

Begin heating the oven to medium. Cut the tomato in half. With a spoon, scoop an area out of each side just large enough to hold one artichoke heart. In a cup, mix the bread crumbs and oil and press half of the crumb mixture onto each tomato/artichoke half. Bake for 20 minutes. Lay a slice of cheese on top and place an olive in the center of the cheese. Bake for another five minutes or until cheese melts, but does not run or burn.

Nutritional information per serving: 332 calories (20.6% from fat), 7.6 g. fat, 27 g. protein, 43.5 g. carbohydrates, 8 mgs. cholesterol.

Of course, you can use your oven to bake bigger vegetables, though they may be too large to cook all at once.

A Sweet Squash

1 small acorn squash (about one pound)
1 orange, peeled and halved
2 tablespoons light brown sugar
2 tablespoons diet margarine

Begin heating the oven to high. Carefully (since it can be fairly difficult) cut the squash in half along its equator. With a spoon, scrape out the seeds. Trim the ends so the squash will remain upright and fit in the oven. Push each orange half into the cavity left after seeding, enlarging the cavity as needed. Divide the sugar and margarine evenly and place on top of the oranges. Cover the exposed side with foil. Bake for 40 minutes or until the squash flesh pierces easily with a fork.

Nutritional information per serving: 345 calories (12% from fat), 4.6 g. fat, 4 g. protein, 78.9 g. carbohydrates, no cholesterol.

Non-Feathered Friends

Dinner on the hoof has always been the oven's specialty. Whether your taste runs to rich-flavored casseroles or the distinctive taste of a seasoned roast, the oven offers a sort of culinary "affirmative action," equalizing the playing field for both the well-to-do and the frugal trekker. Beef can, of course, be lean and tough or fatty and tender. Given a choice, the low-fat chef will opt for the "lesser" cut to keep the fat content down.

Odd thing is, at least when it comes to burger, the leaner the beef, the more expensive the meat. Some of these recipes may put a bigger dent in your food dollar when they suggest using 95%-lean meat. But, consider the extra calories the cheaper cuts deliver. That's not worth any amount of savings!

Shepherd's Pie-Lite

2 large potatoes, peeled and sliced thin
water
salt
2 tablespoons soft diet margarine
¼ cup skim milk (prepared from instant)
8 ounces 95%-lean ground beef
salt and pepper to taste
2 tablespoon all-purpose flour
¼ cup water
2 carrots, scraped, trimmed and chopped
1 rib celery, strings removed and chopped
1 medium onion, chopped

Use your oven pan as a pot. Place the potatoes in salted water to cover, place the pan over a high flame and bring to a boil. Reduce the flame to medium and cook for 15 minutes. Drain the water. Mash the potatoes with the margarine and milk. Remove from the pan and set aside. Clean the pan. Add the ground beef to the non-stick oven pan and place over a medium flame. Cook until the beef loses its pink color and is crumbly. Reduce the heat and add the salt, pepper, flour and water. Stir to make a gravy. Remove from the flame. Stir in the vegetables.

Heat the oven to medium. Spread the mashed potatoes over the meat and vegetable mixture. Place in the oven and bake for 35 minutes.

Nutritional information per serving: 965 calories (14.9% from fat), 16.1 g. fat, 63 g. protein, 142.2 g. carbohydrates, 125 mgs. cholesterol.

Steak In A Blanket

¼ cup all-purpose flour
½ teaspoon salt
¼ teaspoon pepper
8 ounces round steak, trimmed of all visible fat and cut 1½ inches thick
2 teaspoons canola oil
1 medium onion, chopped
1 sweet green pepper, chopped
1 rib celery, strings removed and chopped
¼ cup seedless raisins
2 medium tomatoes, cores removed and cut into chunks

Mix the flour, salt, and pepper together and rub into the steak. Place the non-stick oven pan over a medium flame and add the canola oil. Add the steak and brown on both sides. Remove the pan from the flame.

Heat the oven to medium. Add the remaining ingredients to the steak in the non-stick oven pan. Cover and bake for one to one-and-a-half hours. Turn the steak every 20 minutes.

Suggestion: Warm some bread, wrapped in foil, on the top rack of the oven during the last ten minutes of baking.

Nutritional information per serving: 682 calories (19.1% from fat), 14.5 g. fat, 54 g. protein, 84.4 g. carbohydrates, 134 mgs. cholesterol.

Onusual Onion

   1 large onion
   8 ounces 95%-lean ground beef
   1 tablespoon smooth fat-reduced peanut butter
   ¼ teaspoon ground black pepper
   ⅛ teaspoon ground nutmeg
   1 beef bouillon cube
   1 cup hot water
   1 (8-ounce) can tomatoes
   ¼ cup chopped mushrooms
   2 tablespoons nonfat sour cream
   2 tablespoons Madeira wine

Heat the oven to medium. Cut the onion in half and remove the center, leaving a cup. Trim the bottoms of each half so they will remain upright.

In a bowl, mix together the ground beef, peanut butter, pepper and nutmeg. Stuff the onion halves with the mixture. Place the onions, stuffing side up, in the non-stick oven pan. Dissolve the bouillon cube in the water and pour into the pan with half the tomatoes. Bake for one hour.

While the onions are cooking, mince the onion centers. Once the baking is finished, combine the mushrooms, onion, remaining tomatoes, sour cream and wine in your Sierra cup and heat over the stove to make a sauce. Pour over the baked stuffed onion and serve.

Nutritional information per serving: 600 calories (26.2% from fat), 17.5 g. fat, 56 g. protein, 44.9 g. carbohydrates, 128 mgs. cholesterol.

Fire Breathin' Steak

1 teaspoon olive oil
¼ cup chopped green onion
1 sweet green pepper, cored and sliced
1 large tomato, core removed and the meat chopped
8 ounces top round steak, cut into strips
1 clove garlic, minced
1 teaspoon chili powder
½ teaspoon salt

Add the oil to the non-stick oven pan and place over a medium flame. Add the onion, garlic, green pepper and tomato to the pan and cook until tender, about five to six minutes. Add the round steak and remove the pan from the flame. Begin heating the oven to medium. Stir in the chili powder and salt. Cover and bake for 35 to 40 minutes.

Nutritional information per serving: 381 calories (29% from fat), 12.3 g. fat, 54 g. protein, 13.1 g. carbohydrates, 128 mgs. cholesterol.

Atsa-Nice Pot Roast

2 tablespoons nonfat Italian salad dressing
8 ounces beef top round, trimmed of all visible fat
1 teaspoon olive oil
½ cup water
1 medium onion, peeled and sliced
2 carrots, scraped and sliced
1 large potato, scrubbed and cut into chunks
2 teaspoons cornstarch
2 tablespoons water

Rub the Italian dressing on all sides of the roast. Add the olive oil to the non-stick oven pan and place over a medium flame. Add the roast and brown on all sides. Remove the pan from the flame.

Heat the oven to medium. Add the water and vegetables to the roast in the non-stick oven pan. Place in oven and bake for one hour. Take the meat from pan and place on a serving plate.

In a cup, mix the cornstarch and water until the cornstarch dissolves. Place the pan over a medium flame and stir in the cornstarch mixture. When the liquid comes to a boil, remove the pan from the flame. Pour the gravy and vegetables over the meat.

Nutritional information per serving: 689 calories (15.9% from fat), 12.2 g. fat, 59 g. protein, 83.8 g. carbohydrates, 128 mgs. cholesterol.

Lasagna a la Kate

8 ounces 95%-lean ground beef
6 ounces lasagna noodles, pre-cooked
1 cup nonfat spaghetti sauce
½ cup reduced-fat ricotta cheese
2 tablespoons grated Parmesan cheese

Add the ground beef to the non-stick oven pan and place over a medium flame. Brown and break up the beef. Stir in the spaghetti sauce. Remove the pan from the flame and remove the sauce from the pan.

Begin heating the oven to medium. In a separate bowl, stir together the cheeses. Place a single layer of the noodles on the bottom of the non-stick oven pan. Next, put down a layer of cheese, followed by a layer of meat sauce, then another layer of noodles...and so forth until you run out of noodles. (You may have to cut the lasagna noodles in half to accommodate the size of the oven pan.) Bake for 35 to 40 minutes. Serves two.

Nutritional information per serving: 619 calories (19.5% from fat), 13.5 g. fat, 45.5 g. protein, 76.3 g. carbohydrates, 85 mgs. cholesterol.

Boeuf n' All

2 tablespoons all-purpose flour
1 tablespoon prepared (yellow) mustard
salt and ground black pepper to taste
8 ounces beef top round, trimmed of all visible fat and cut into bite-sized pieces
1 teaspoon canola oil
1 medium onion, peeled and diced
1 beef bouillon cube
1 cup hot water
1 large potato, scrubbed and sliced thin
¼ cup nonfat sour cream

Add the flour, mustard, salt and pepper to a bowl and stir together until combined. Add the beef to the bowl and stir until coated. Add the oil to the non-stick oven pan and place over a medium flame. Add the coated beef to the pan and cook, stirring, until it begins to brown. Add the onions and cook until tender, about six minutes. Remove the pan from the flame.

Heat the oven to medium. In a cup, dissolve the bouillon in the water and pour over the beef. Add and stir in the potatoes. Bake for 45 minutes. Just before serving, stir in the sour cream.

Suggestion: Fresh carrot sticks and warm rolls make this a meal fit for an elegant dining table.

Nutritional information per serving: 726 calories (16.6% from fat), 13.4 g. fat, 61 g. protein, 84.2 g. carbohydrates, 132 mgs. cholesterol.

Paprika'd Beef Stew

> 1 teaspoon canola oil
> 8 ounces beef sirloin tip, trimmed of all visible fat and cut into small cubes
> 1 medium onion, chopped
> 1 beef bouillon cube
> 1 cup hot water
> 1 teaspoon sweet paprika
> ¼ teaspoon caraway seeds
> 1 (6-ounce) can tomato paste
> 2 medium potatoes, scrubbed and cut into cubes

Add the oil to the non-stick oven pan and place over a medium flame. Add the cubed beef and cook, stirring until browned. Reduce the flame to low and add the onions. Cook, stirring, until the onions are softened, about five minutes. Remove the pan from the flame.

Heat the oven to medium. In a cup, mix the bouillon cube and water until dissolved. Add it and the paprika, caraway seeds and tomato paste to the pot and stir until well combined. Cover and bake for one hour. Add the potatoes and return to the oven for 30 minutes.

Suggestion: Serve with warm hard rolls.

Nutritional information per serving: 867 calories (15.9% from fat), 15.3 g. fat, 62 g. protein, 124.7 g. carbohydrates, 134 mgs. cholesterol.

There are many flavorful and lean cuts of beef that cry out for a smart chef to turn them into a toothsome meal. Try a few of these favorites on your next trek.

Flank steak can be one tough piece of beef unless properly sliced. Flank steak should be cut across the grain into thin slices. Doing so will render a very tender and tasty piece of meat.

"Watch-Your-Flank" Baked Beef

2 tablespoons clover honey
2 tablespoons barbecue sauce
1 teaspoon olive oil
1 tablespoon lemon juice
8 ounces beef flank steak, trimmed of all visible fat
1 large onion, peeled and cut into chunks
1 sweet red pepper, cored and seeds removed, sliced
2 cups pre-cooked noodles

Heat the oven to medium/high. In a cup, stir together the honey, barbecue sauce, oil and lemon juice to make a sauce. Rub the sauce into the steak and let the steak rest in the sauce for ten to 15 minutes. Place the steak in the non-stick oven pan and surround with the vegetables. Pour remaining sauce over all. Bake for 15 to 20 minutes. Serve with the reheated noodles. Serves two.

Nutritional information per serving: 522 calories (20.4% from fat), 11.8 g. fat, 29.5 g. protein, 71.4 g. carbohydrates, 56 mgs. cholesterol.

"Aye, There's The Rub" Flank Steak

½ teaspoon each salt and ground black pepper
½ teaspoon sweet paprika
¼ teaspoon garlic powder
6 ounce beef flank steak, trimmed of all visible fat
1 medium onion, sliced
½ cup rehydrated freeze-dried corn, drained

In a cup, combine the salt, pepper, paprika and garlic powder. Sprinkle the flank steak with the spice mixture and rub it into both sides. Set aside for 15 minutes.

Heat the oven to high. Scatter the onion across the bottom of the non-stick oven pan. Place the flank steak on top. Cover and bake for 15 minutes. Spoon the corn on the steak and return to the oven for five minutes.

Suggestion: Adding a little steak sauce to the meat really beefs this up.

Nutritional information per serving: 398 calories (29.8% from fat), 13.2 g. fat, 36 g. protein, 31.5 g. carbohydrates, 85 mgs. cholesterol.

Classic Roast Beef Lite

1 tablespoon Kitchen Bouquet®
8 ounce beef eye of the round roast
1 teaspoon each ground black pepper and dried thyme
½ teaspoon salt
1 medium russet (baking) potato, cut in half

Heat the oven to very high. Rub the Kitchen Bouquet® (available in spice/gravy sections of most grocery stores) all over the roast. In a cup, stir together the pepper, thyme and salt. Sprinkle all over the roast. Place the roast in the oven pan. Bake for 15 minutes.

Wrap the baking potato in foil. Reduce the oven heat to medium and place the potato on the top oven rack. Continue baking for one hour.

Nutritional information per serving: 516 calories (17.1% from fat), 9.8 g. fat, 54 g. protein, 51 g. carbohydrates, 121 mgs. cholesterol.

What-A-Filet

2 beef filets, about 1½ inches thick
1 teaspoon celery salt
2 large stuffing mushrooms
¼ cup fat-free Swiss cheese, shredded
2 tablespoons minced spinach leaves
2 tablespoons seasoned bread crumbs
1 teaspoon olive oil
4 slices fat-free Swiss cheese

Heat the oven to medium. Season both sides of each filet with the celery salt. Set aside. In a bowl, mix together the grated cheese, spinach, bread crumbs and oil. Remove the stems of mushrooms. Carefully cut off part of the top of the cap to make a flat surface. Stuff the mushrooms with the cheese mixture.

Place the filets in the non-stick oven pan and bake for about 15 minutes. Place one mushroom on top of each filet and continue baking for another five minutes. Top each filet with a slice of the cheese and continue baking for one minute more, or until the cheese just begins to melt.

Nutritional information per serving: 529 calories (23.3% from fat), 13.7 g. fat, 72 g. protein, 23.8 g. carbohydrates, 132 mgs. cholesterol.

Other Meats, Etc.

As the ads say, pork is "the other white" meat. Well-trimmed pork is a super-lean option for the low-fat trekker. It's also true that you can make a variety of super casseroles in your oven.

Fungi Chops

½ teaspoon canola oil
2 very lean, center-cut pork loin chops (8 ounces total) boned and trimmed of all visible fat
1 packet Lipton Cup-A-Soup® cream of mushroom soup mix and water to prepare
chopped parsley leaves
1 large potato, scrubbed and sliced

Add the oil to the non-stick oven pan and place over a medium flame. Add the pork chops and lightly brown on both sides. Remove the pan from the flame.

Heat the oven to medium. Pour the prepared mushroom soup over the pork chops. Sprinkle the parsley over all. Lay the potato slices around the edge of the pan. Cover and bake for 45 minutes.

Nutritional information per serving: 672 calories (22.7% from fat), 17 g. fat, 57.3 g. protein, 70.3 g. carbohydrates, 143 mgs. cholesterol.

Roast Pork 'n Apples

1 tablespoon light brown sugar
8 ounce boneless pork loin roast, trimmed of all visible fat
1 medium apple, cored and chopped
½ cup applesauce
2 tablespoons light brown sugar
1 teaspoon ground cinnamon
½ teaspoon ground nutmeg
1 cup pre-cooked white or brown rice

Heat the oven to medium.

Rub the tablespoon of brown sugar all over the roast. Place the roast in – the non-stick oven pan. Bake for 45 minutes. While the roast is baking, combine the apple, applesauce, two tablespoons of brown sugar and spices. Add to the roast, covering the meat with the mixture. Cover and bake for 45 minutes more. Wrap the rice in a foil packet and place on the upper oven rack during the last ten minutes.

Suggestion: Serve with a relish tray of pickles, olives, pickled beets and celery sticks. This is an easy meal that will fill you up.

Nutritional information per serving: 759 calories (15% from fat), 12.6 g. fat, 54 g. protein, 107 g. carbohydrates, 143 mgs. cholesterol.

Double B Ranch Q-Ribs

   8 ounces very lean farmer-style pork ribs (2), trimmed of all fat
   ½ cup barbecue sauce (your choice, but to us, spicier is better)
   1 medium onion, peeled and cut into chunks
   1 cup precooked white or brown rice

Heat the oven to medium.Place the ribs in the oven pan and pour the barbecue sauce over all. Use the onions to keep the ribs from touching the side of the pan. Bake for 45 minutes to one hour. About ten minutes before ribs are finished, add the rice to the oven pan to heat.

Nutritional information per serving: 675 calories (18.7% from fat), 14 g. fat, 56 g. protein, 74 g. carbohydrates, 143 mgs. cholesterol.

Deep Dish Italian Sausage Spaghetti

   ½ teaspoon olive oil
   8 ounces very lean turkey Italian sausage
   1 (8-ounce) can tomato sauce
   ¼ teaspoon each dried oregano and basil, crumbled
   ¼ teaspoon each garlic powder and fennel seed
   1 teaspoon granulated sugar
   1 teaspoon grated Parmesan cheese
   1 medium bay leaf
   1 medium onion, peeled and chopped
   1 large sweet green pepper, core and seeds removed, sliced
   1 medium zucchini squash, trimmed and sliced
   2 ounces grated nonfat mozzarella cheese
   1¼ cups pre-cooked spaghetti or other pasta

Place the non-stick oven pan over a medium flame and add the oil. Add the Italian sausage and cook until browned, five to six minutes. In a bowl, stir the tomato sauce with the oregano, basil, garlic powder, fennel seed, sugar, Parmesan cheese and bay leaf. Remove the oven pan from the flame. Begin heating the oven to medium.

Add the vegetables to the oven pan and pour the sauce over all. Distribute the mozzarella cheese over the top and bake for 35 to 40 minutes. Serve over the pre-cooked pasta.

Nutritional information per serving: 867 calories (17% from fat), 16.4 g. fat, 79 g. protein, 104 g. carbohydrates, 137 mgs. cholesterol.

Pineapple Pork

  8 ounces ground pork tenderloin
  ½ teaspoon salt
  1 small Vidalia (or other sweet) onion, peeled and diced
  1 medium sweet red pepper, core and seeds removed, diced
  ¼ teaspoon dry mustard
  ¼ cup nonfat egg substitute
  ½ cup bread crumbs
  ½ cup canned crushed pineapple, drained

Heat the oven to medium. In a bowl, combine all the ingredients. Turn into the non-stick oven pan, forming a loaf. Bake for 45 minutes.

Suggestion: Serve with fresh, sliced yellow summer squash.

Nutritional information per serving: 649 calories (15.5% from fat), 11.2 g. fat, 62 g. protein, 70 g. carbohydrates, 147 mgs. cholesterol.

Southern Style Ham

  8 ounces 95%-lean (or leaner) canned ham
  8 whole cloves
  2 tablespoons light brown sugar
  1 medium sweet potato, scrubbed and cut into quarters
  1 tablespoon diet margarine
  1 cup pre-cooked brown or white rice, wrapped in foil

Heat the oven to medium. Place the ham in the non-stick oven pan. Push the cloves into the ham, evenly distributed across the top. Sprinkle the brown sugar on top of the ham. Place the sweet potato around the ham, skin side down. Place a dab of margarine on each sweet potato. Cover and bake for one hour and 15 minutes. During the last ten minutes, place the foil-wrapped rice on the top oven rack.

Nutritional information per serving: 698 calories (16% from fat), 12.4 g. fat, 50 g. protein, 92.4 g. carbohydrates, 104 mgs. cholesterol.

Corn Pone Pork Pie

  1 (1-ounce) packet brown gravy mix
  ¼ cup minced Canadian bacon
  1 large cooked potato, sliced thin

1 medium onion, peeled, trimmed and diced
1 cup cooked pork tenderloin, diced
salt and pepper to taste
½ teaspoon sage, crumbled
1 (8.5-ounce) package instant corn muffin mix
¼ cup nonfat egg substitute
⅓ cup skim milk

Prepare the brown gravy mix per packet directions, in a cup over a medium to low flame. Set aside. Heat the oven to medium. Scatter the bacon across the bottom of the non-stick oven pan. Distribute the potato and onion on top of the bacon. In a bowl, mix the pork with the salt, pepper and sage. Top the vegetables with this mixture. Pour the gravy over all, cover and bake for 40 minutes.

In a bowl, prepare the corn muffin mix with the egg substitute and milk. Remove the oven pan from the oven, uncover and pour the muffin mix batter over the pan's ingredients, smoothing out to the edge. Return the pan, uncovered, to the oven for 20 minutes. Serves two.

Nutritional information per serving: 825 calories (20.5% from fat), 18.8 g. fat, 35.5 g. protein, 125.3 g. carbohydrates, 55 mgs. cholesterol.

Here's a family favorite...sort of a ham-and-cheese sandwich dressed up for dinner. (No bread, hold the high-fat mayo, please!)

Cheesy Spuds 'n Ham

½ cup skim (prepared from instant)
½ cup reduced-fat cheddar cheese, shredded
2 tablespoons all-purpose flour
1 cup diced lean baked ham
2 medium potatoes, peeled and sliced thin
1 medium onion, sliced
4 tablespoons bread crumbs

Add the skim milk to the non-stick oven pan and place over a medium-low flame. Heat to near boiling. Stir in the cheese and flour and remove the pan from the flame.

Heat the oven to medium. Add the ham, potatoes and onions to the oven pan, stirring to mix well. Sprinkle the bread crumbs over the top and bake for 45 minutes.

Nutritional information per serving: 910 calories (16.8% from fat), 17 g. fat, 57 g. protein, 130.4 g. carbohydrates, 54 mgs. cholesterol.

Shirley May's Tuna Noodle Bake

1 cup pre-cooked egg noodles
1 (6.75-ounce) can water-packed albacore tuna, drained and
   flaked
1 packet Lipton Cup-A-Soup® cream of mushroom soup mix and
   water to prepare
¼ cup chopped fresh parsley leaves
1 tablespoon diet margarine, melted
2 tablespoons bread crumbs

Heat the oven to medium. In the non-stick oven pan, mix together the
noodles, tuna, soup mix, water and parsley until combined. Drizzle the
melted margarine over the top. Sprinkle the bread crumbs over all.
Bake, uncovered, for 35 minutes.

*Nutritional information per serving: 588 calories (16.2% from fat), 10.6 g. fat,
56.3 g. protein, 62.3 g. carbohydrates, 138 mgs. cholesterol.*

Baked Goods

Probably the easiest way to bake on the trail is to use pre-packaged
rolls from a grocery store. They keep a day or so without refrigeration, but must be chilled somewhat before you set out. Use frozen
meat to keep them cool until you are ready to bake.

Pre-packaged refrigerated rolls, however, can be very high in fat
content, often exceeding 50% of the calories. Check the food fact
label and select ones that are comparatively low in fat.

There are great ways to stay low fat if you start from scratch.

Lean D's Biscuits

½ cup all-purpose flour
½ teaspoon baking powder
⅛ teaspoon salt
1 teaspoon canola oil
¼ cup water

Heat the oven to medium. Combine all the ingredients, adding just
enough water to make a good stiff dough. Flour your hands and make
biscuits about two inches in diameter and one inch thick. Place the biscuits in the non-stick oven pan and bake for ten to 15 minutes, check-
ing to make certain they do not over-brown.

*Nutritional information per serving: 267 calories (17.2% from fat), 5.1 g. fat,
6 g. protein, 47.9 g. carbohydrates, no cholesterol.*

Corn Bread Lite

¾ cup all-purpose flour
⅓ cup yellow cornmeal
2 tablespoons granulated sugar
⅛ teaspoon salt
1 teaspoon baking powder
¼ cup nonfat egg substitute
½ cup skim milk (prepared from instant)
2 tablespoons drained, unsweetened applesauce
canola oil

Begin heating the oven to high. In a bowl, stir together all the dry ingredients. Add the wet ingredients and stir until just combined. Do not over-mix. Lightly oil the non-stick oven pan and add the corn bread batter. Bake for 25 minutes, watching to make sure that the bread does not burn. Cut into wedges. Serves two.

Suggestion: If you can find them, pack in single-serving packets of honey. The honey is great drizzled over fresh, warm corn bread.

Nutritional information per serving: 345 calories (3.7% from fat), 1.4 g. fat, 11.5 g. protein, 70.7 g. carbohydrates, 1 mg. cholesterol.

Lite Southern-Style Hush Puppies

1 cup yellow cornmeal
½ teaspoon salt
½ teaspoon baking powder
¼ cup nonfat egg substitute
½ cup skim milk (prepared from instant)
1 tablespoon minced onion
canola oil

Heat the oven to high. In a bowl, stir together the dry ingredients until combined. Add egg substitute, milk and onion. Mix together to form a dough. Form into half-inch oblong patties and place in the non-stick oven pan. Lightly brush with the oil and bake for ten to 15 minutes or until nicely browned. Serves two.

Nutritional information per serving: 291 calories (5.4% from fat), 1.8 g. fat, 11 g. protein, 57 g. carbohydrates, 1 mgs. cholesterol.

Shortcake means shortened cake. Does that mean it shrank? No–it means lots of shortening (butter, oil or lard) has been added. It certainly made a light, flaky cake, but the fat was way too high.

DM went to his lean kitchen and created this recipe, which includes canola oil (the lowest in saturated fat) and drained applesauce.

Shortcake Biscuits

1 cup all-purpose flour
1½ teaspoons baking powder
1½ tablespoons granulated sugar
¼ teaspoon salt
¼ cup nonfat egg substitute
⅓ cup skim milk (prepared from instant)
1 tablespoon canola oil
1 tablespoon drained unsweetened applesauce

Heat the oven to high. In a bowl, stir together the dry ingredients until combined. Add the wet ingredients and work together until it makes a stiff dough. (If the dough seems too loose, add flour as needed.) Coat your hands with flour and make biscuits about a half to three-quarter of an inch thick and three inches across. Bake for 15 minutes. Serves two.

Nutritional information per serving: 353 calories (18.6% from fat), 7.3 g. fat, 10.5 g. protein, 60.6 g. carbohydrates, no cholesterol.

The End Of The Trail

After-dinner delights can enhance your evenings when you've got your oven along. The oven lets you eat cake...or baked fruits...or even gingerbread. Taste-tempting toppers to low-fat meals don't have to be diet busters, either.

The following lite dessert recipes will make that last cup of coffee after a hard day on the trail a most satisfying experience.

Hint: When using the Outback Oven to bake desserts, keep a close watch on the temperature reading. Keep it on the "k" in bake by adjusting the flame on the stove accordingly. This level of heat within the pan is equivalent to a medium (350˚) oven. You should, therefore, be able to follow the times given with the recipes. With a homemade oven, you can lift the lid to test cakes with a toothpick. With the Outback Oven you have to fly blind, because once you lift the lid, you're done.

Less Is More Gingerbread

1 cup all-purpose flour
½ teaspoon baking soda
½ teaspoon each ground cinnamon and ground ginger
¼ teaspoon each ground cloves and salt
¼ cup drained unsweetened applesauce
¼ cup nonfat egg substitute
⅓ cup molasses
½ cup hot water
¼ cup granulated sugar
¼ cup seedless raisins
canola oil

Heat the oven to medium. In a bowl, stir together all the dry ingredients until combined. In a separate bowl, stir together the wet ingredients plus the sugar and raisins. Add the dry ingredients to the wet ingredients and stir until just moistened. Pour into a lightly oiled non-stick oven pan and bake for 45 minutes. Cut into wedges. Serves four.

Nutritional information per serving: 360 calories (2% from fat), 0.8 g. fat, 5.8 g. protein, 86.2 g. carbohydrates, no cholesterol.

Divine Apples

2 medium apples (Macintosh is best), cored and sliced thin
2 tablespoons dark brown sugar
½ teaspoon ground cinnamon
¼ teaspoon ground
2 teaspoons diet margarine

Heat the oven to medium. Distribute the apple slices evenly across the bottom of the non-stick oven pan. Sprinkle the brown sugar and spices over the apples. Place dots of the margarine all around. Cover and bake for 20 minutes.

Nutritional information per serving: 225 calories (8.4% from fat), 2.1 g. fat, trace of protein, 55.2 g. carbohydrates, no cholesterol.

Grandma's Coffee Cake

Cake:
¼ cup light brown sugar
2 teaspoons ground cinnamon
½ cup skim milk (prepared from instant)
¼ cup nonfat egg substitute
1 cup Bisquick® reduced-fat baking mix
Topping:
½ cup dark brown sugar
1 tablespoon diet margarine

Heat the oven to medium. In a bowl, stir the sugar, cinnamon, milk and nonfat egg substitute. Gradually add the Bisquick and stir until the batter becomes smooth. Pour the batter into the non-stick oven pan.

In a cup, mix the topping ingredients together until they are crumbly. Sprinkle over the top of the coffee cake batter. Bake for 25 minutes or until a toothpick inserted in the center of coffee cake comes out clean. Cut into wedges and serve. Serves four.

Nutritional information per serving: 253 calories (9.5% from fat), 2.7 g. fat, 5 g. protein, 52.4 g. carbohydrates, 1 mgs. cholesterol.

Blueberry Cobbler

½ cup blueberries (thinly sliced apples may successfully be substituted)
¼ teaspoon ground cinnamon
¼ teaspoons ground nutmeg
¼ teaspoon all-purpose flour
1 cup Bisquick® reduced-fat baking mix
2 tablespoons diet margarine, melted
¼ cup granulated sugar
¼ cup nonfat egg substitute
¼ cup skim milk (prepared from instant)

Heat the oven to medium. Add the blueberries, spices and flour to the bottom of the non-stick oven pan and stir until coated. In a bowl, stir together the remaining ingredients and pour over the fruit mixture. Bake for 25 minutes or until the top is browned. Serve warm. Serves four.

Nutritional information per serving: 211 calories (13.5% from fat), 3.2 g. fat, 5.3 g. protein, 40.3 g. carbohydrates, trace of cholesterol.

Afterword

Our tour of the low-fat meal horizon has brought us full circle, back to the plate, which from the start is what we wanted to fill.

Whether cooked in the skillet, the pot or the oven, One Pan meals can be exciting, nutritious and low-fat. Now, we'd like to let you in on a few of our absolute favorite recipes...the ones we frequently cook trailside for ourselves or our families.

In the skillet:

Green Eggs, No Ham...Ma'am
Chicken Paprika
Lite 'N Saucy Chicken
Basil's Full Meal Chicken
Lean On Me Chili
Thai-Hi Beef

In the pot:

Nana's Eggs a la Golden Rod
Pepper Pot Chicken
Big Red Bird
Savoyard Roast
Biftek Ratatouille
Indian Corn Pudding

In the oven:

Dutchman's Wundercake
Blue Plate Chicken
The One Pan Gourmet Lite Pizza
Shepherd's Pie-Lite
Classic Roast Beef
Less Is More Gingerbread

INDEX